Micro Markets Workbook

Micro Markets Workbook

*A Market Structure Approach to
Microeconomic Analysis*

ROBERT A. SCHWARTZ

MICHAEL G. CAREW

TATIANA MAKSIMENKO

WILEY

John Wiley & Sons, Inc.

For Our Daughters
Emily, Alicia, and Karen

Contents

Preface

This workbook provides readers of *Micro Markets* with a convenient means of reviewing material presented in the text, and of enhancing their understanding of the principles of microeconomic theory. It is designed for use in advanced undergraduate and graduate presentations of microeconomics.

Microeconomics is the study of the behavior of individuals and households as they make consumption and production decisions and interact with each other in a micro market. A micro market is the market for a specific good, service, factor of production, or asset (e.g., books, haircuts, dentists, a house, a factory, or shares of a firm's common stock).

The study of the detailed operations of a micro market (e.g., how orders are submitted, handled, and turned into trades) is called *market microstructure*. Microstructure analysis, a relatively new field in financial economics, has to date been applied to financial markets with a specific focus on equity markets. Being based on microeconomic principles, equity market microstructure is indeed a good application of much traditional microeconomic theory, and it is used to this end in the Micro Markets textbook. We trust that the microstructure application will underscore for you the applicability of microeconomics to a wide range of issues that we face regarding real-world markets.

And so, *Micro Markets* turns to the equities markets as a consistent application of microeconomic theory. This workbook, while also referring to the equities markets, expands the application of microeconomic principles to other markets. We also underscore several realities of markets that are stressed in *Micro Markets*. Real-world markets are not perfectly liquid, frictionless environments. Rather, they are replete with trading costs and blockages. The information sets that agents base their decisions on can be enormous, complex, incomplete, and imprecise. An array of other factors ranging from dishonest and irrational behavior to principal-agent problems and systemic risk perturb the allocational efficiency of a competitive, frictionless, free market environment. Occasionally, the micro markets suffer through widespread, macroeconomic downturns. In the latter chapters of the text and here in the workbook we consider the events that constitute the financial crisis of 2007–2009 as both an example and a test of market based microeconomic theory. All of this raises a fundamental question of the role that government should play in regulating and otherwise controlling micro markets. This workbook should give you further food for thought concerning this vitally important issue.

The workbook provides a convenient track for both simultaneous use while reading *Micro Markets*, and as a study vehicle for summarizing the course. Each of its eight chapters focuses on its corresponding chapter in the textbook. Each chapter in the workbook comprises eight sections that permit the student to anticipate the textual reading as well as subsequent review. The workbook chapter sections are:

1. Learning objectives for the chapter.
2. Chapter summary.
3. Glossary of terms employed in the chapter.
4. Current events reports that illustrate the chapter concepts and attendant questions.
5. Multiple-choice review questions.
6. Applications and issues.
7. Recommended readings for further research.
8. Answers to the multiple-choice review questions.

Throughout, our intention is also for this workbook to be a convenient and thought-provoking resource for classroom discussion and assignments.

CHAPTER 1

Introduction to Market-Driven Economics

LEARNING OBJECTIVES

- **Understand what microeconomics is all about.** Economics is the study of how societies allocate their scarce resources among competing needs. You should also begin to appreciate the role that market architecture plays in the operations of a marketplace.
- **Understand why scarcity implies trade-offs.** Because individuals (and societies) do not possess unlimited resources, scarcity exists. In choosing both broad economic goals and specific goods and services, societies and individuals curtail their pursuit of some goals or goods/services in order to obtain more of others. In other words, to obtain more of one goal or good/service, the decision maker *must* settle for less of some other goal or good/service. This trade-off lies at the heart of an economic problem.
- **Start to become acquainted with the equities markets and how trades occur.** Buyers and sellers of equity securities (common stock) come together to trade in an equities market. Buyers and sellers have differing estimates about the future value of various stocks, and also different cash flow needs. The buyers and sellers make their purchases and sales based on their individual needs and estimates of future values.
- **Identify the topics covered in microeconomics.** Microeconomics is the study of how individual economic units (households and firms) determine both what and how many goods and services to consume and to produce, respectively. Households' consumption decisions are made in light of their evaluations of the satisfaction (utility) that they receive from the different goods and services that they consume. Firms' production decisions are based upon their technological capabilities and the

cost of obtaining the factors of production which are provided to them by households and other firms.

- **Identify the costs that matter in making decisions.** While consumers seek goods and services that provide them with the highest satisfaction (utility), their consumption is limited by their available income and wealth, and by the cost of the resources that they wish to acquire. Similarly, producers consider consumers' appetites for goods and services, and will not produce units of a good/service when the cost of obtaining them exceeds the value of what they produce to consumers.

- **Understand the use of marginal analysis for making decisions.** Consumers and producers are rational. They assess the cost and satisfaction (utility) of each additional unit of consumption or production. When the cost of producing *an additional unit* exceeds the consumers' appetite *on the margin*, total satisfaction (utility) must decline and production/consumption should be curtailed. On the other hand, if the cost of *an additional unit* is less than the consumers' utility *on the margin*, total production/consumption should be increased.

- **Understand the different ways of classifying and measuring costs.** Costs are classified as either fixed or variable. In the short run some costs are fixed; in the long run all costs are variable. The cost of any output can be measured as total cost, average cost, and/or marginal cost.

- **Why markets are a good, but not a perfect, way to allocate resources.** There are several different methods of allocating scarce resources including coercion, moral authority, and privilege. Free markets tend to achieve an efficient allocation of scarce resources across their alternative uses. Free markets, however, can also fail to achieve textbook efficient results. The chapter introduces you to an array of causes of market failure that are returned to in later chapters of the book.

CHAPTER SUMMARY

In this introductory chapter we establish several key learning goals and concepts that will be themes in our market structure presentation of microeconomics. Here are some highlights:

1. Microeconomics is the study of how economic units determine what and how many goods and services to consume (households) and produce (firms), and what and how much of the factors of production (labor and capital) to supply (households) and to use in production (firms).
2. Microeconomic theory formalizes basic principles concerning how best to resolve the trade-offs involved in consumption, production, and

other allocation decisions. It does so by tying assumptions together to form an economic model. The assumptions individually need not be perfect reflections of real-world economic activity. Theory, by its nature, is abstract, while real-world markets can be very intricate. The hallmark of a good theory is that, although abstract, it provides insights that enable us to understand better the operations of the real-world, micro markets.

3. Market structure refers to the architectural realities of actual marketplaces. These encompass the institutional features that pertain to market design and operations.

4. The power of microeconomic theory can be better understood by applying it to an actual, real-world market. Throughout the book, as we extend our theoretical discussion to a nonfrictionless market characterized by imperfect information, trading costs and blockages, we focus on the equity markets. Specifically, we consider the secondary markets where already issued equity shares trade (not the primary markets where new shares are issued).

5. Equity market microstructure, a relatively new field in financial economics, considers the processes by which orders are submitted to a nonfrictionless marketplace, are handled in the marketplace, and are turned into trades and transaction prices.

6. Market participants (buyers-consumers and sellers-producers) interact to set the prices of goods and services in the context of specific institutional environments. Through price setting, markets allocate scarce resources to participants according to the relative prices that they face, their incomes (or wealth positions), and their tastes for the various goods and services as described by their utility functions (and also by technology which is described by production functions, a topic that we discuss in Chapter 5).

7. A vast array of different markets exists, including commodities (such as coal, crude oil, wheat, and wood), labor (full-time and part-time), managerial resources, and capital (physical and financial.) Equities markets (one of the markets for financial capital) are an excellent target for market microstructure analysis.

8. We have addressed the question, how well do markets function? On one hand, there is the positive force exerted by Adam Smith's invisible hand. On the other hand, the forces of competition that the invisible hand represents are impeded by some agents having market power (at the extreme, monopoly power), and by various other factors including trading costs, imperfect information, and systemic risk.

9. To understand better just how prices and transactions' volumes are determined in an equity market based on the order-flow received by the

market, and to appreciate that trading in an equity market involves making tactical decisions, we have noted that the market can be thought of as an ecology. Traders interact with each other for a multiplicity of motives, and a multiplicity of motives is, in fact, required for an equity market to operate effectively.

10. We have presented seven key concepts: *ceteris paribus*, fixed costs versus variable costs and return, long-run versus short-run analysis, equilibrium, marginal analysis, elasticity, and maximum versus minimum versus optimum. These concepts underlie much of the discussion in the rest of the book. It is important to have a good grasp of them. If you feel comfortable with these concepts you will appreciate your study of this market structure presentation of microeconomics.

GLOSSARY

ceteris paribus   Latin for "other things being equal." A methodological treatment that enables the net effect of one variable (an independent variable) on another variable (a dependent variable) to be obtained while holding all other relevant independent variables constant.

demand curve   A graph of the relationship between the quantity demanded of a good and the price of the good, all else constant.

effective demand   The amount of a good that a buyer actually be willing to purchase.

elasticity   The responsiveness of demand or supply to one of its determinants. For instance, let Y be a dependent variable and X be an independent variable. The elasticity of Y with respect to X is the percentage change in Y divided by the percentage change in X. Perhaps X is the quantity of a good demanded and Y is the unit price of X (own price elasticity). Or Y could be income (income elasticity), or Y could be the price of another good that is related in consumption (cross-price elasticity).

equity market microstructure   The analysis of the detailed way in which orders to trade equity shares are submitted to the market, handled by the market, and turned into trades and transaction prices. Of particular importance is how the design and operation of a specific market permits price discovery and cost containment.

equities   The indicia of ownership in an economic enterprise; typically common stock.

fixed costs   Costs of production that do not vary with output. Fixed costs exist in the short run; in the long run, all costs are variable.

frictional and frictionless   These opposites reflect the realities of market frictions (the costs, blockages, and imperfect information) compared to a theoretical frictionless market without costs and characterized by perfect information.

initial public offering (IPO) The first public sale of equity shares by a previously privately owned enterprise.

liquidity The characteristic of a micro market that permits buyers and sellers to trade reasonably quickly, in reasonable amounts, at reasonable prices. An attribute of the shares of an asset that, along with risk, affect the expected return and hence the price of an asset.

macroeconomics The economics of national or regional production and consumption emphasizing the formulation of economic policies. Macroeconomics stresses the importance of flow variables such as aggregate income, production, employment, and interest rates, while microeconomics stresses the importance of variables such as relative prices.

marginal utility The change of utility obtained from consuming a good or service with respect to the change in the amount of the good or service consumed, all else equal.

marginal values The change in the value of a depend variable with respect to the change in the value of an independent variable. For instance, with the total cost of production being an increasing function of the total amount of a good or service produced, the marginal cost of production is the amount by which the total cost increases as output increases.

market architecture The design of a trading venue, including the rules and regulations that govern trading.

market breakdown (failure) When a specific market fails to achieve an efficient market outcome from a public policy point of view. The failure can be in terms of price established and/or quantity traded. It can be attributable to factors such as externalities, asymmetric information, or moral hazard problems. In the extreme, a market can actually shut down (that is, totally ceases operations).

market efficiency The quality of a market as manifested in liquidity supply, cost containment, and the sharpness of price discovery.

market microstructure The composition and structure of the market for a particular product (good or service).

microeconomic theory The study of how markets operate. A common definition is the analysis of the allocation of scarce resources between competing ends.

microeconomics The economics of household and firm production and consumption of goods and services, and the supply of factors of production.

movements along a curve For instance, the coordinated change in the price of a good and the quantity of the good that is purchased, all else held constant. In contrast, when variables other than the price of the good change, the curve itself changes position.

optimal amount Neither the maximum nor the minimum, an optimal amount is just the right amount. For instance, in a two-good universe (X and Y), the optimum amount is the best quantity of X to consume when more or less of good X can be purchased. For a household, when the inputs of all goods (X, Y, etc.), have been *optimized*, the decision maker's utility has been *maximized*. Similarly, a firm's profits are maximized when its factors of production (labor and capital) are being used in optimal amounts.

primary markets   The market for the offering of new shares of a specific equity (common stock). In secondary market trading, the term is also used to designate the main market where the stock trades when there are several other, smaller markets that orders can be sent to.

secondary markets   The markets where already issued equity shares are traded (for instance, the New York Stock Exchange, NASDAQ, the London Stock Exchange, or Deutsche Börse).

shift of a curve   Consider, for instance, the undefined consumption good, X. Let the demand for X be a function of the price of X, the price of a related good (call it Y), income, and the consumer's tastes as described by a utility function. A change in the price of X with all other relevant variables constant (price of Y, income, and tastes) results in a move along the consumer's demand curve for X. A change in any of the other variables (either the price of Y, income, and/or tastes) with the price of X constant, results in a shift of (not a movement along) the consumer's demand curve for X.

utility value   The value to a consumer of a good or service measured in terms of the pure pleasure obtained (or pain avoided). Utility is an abstract, theoretical concept that is represented by ordinal, not cardinal numbers.

variable costs   The costs of producing a good that vary with the amount of the good produced. In the long run, all costs are variable.

wishful demand   The amount of a good that a buyer would ideally like to consume, but cannot necessarily obtain because he or she does not have the resources to make the purchase.

CURRENT EVENTS DISCUSSIONS

1. Internationally, Markets and Competition Are Viewed Differently. Is Monopoly a Threat to Market Competition?

As we proceed with our examination of the microstructure of markets, we must always keep in mind that different markets for different commodities in different countries have their own individual architectures, participants, rules, and regulators. The focus of our discussion is on the model of the American equities markets, which have evolved over a period of more than 200 years. Not all markets have that length of experience or the volumes and diversity of participants. Therefore, as we go forward using the U.S. equities markets as our model, we should always recognize that the principles we deduce from our observations should be projected with care upon the other markets of the world.

    The following article illustrates the particular views of U.S. and European market regulators toward the issue of "market power" and the prospects of monopoly control of a market.

Oceans Apart

Europe still seems to have less faith than America in the ability of the free market to tame monopolies.

America fosters competition; Europe protects competitors. That jeer is tossed across the Atlantic pretty frequently. Watchdogs on both sides of the ocean play down the idea that the Europeans bite more often than the Americans. But although the gap is far narrower than it was a few years ago, it still exists. The commission (the European Union's antitrust authority) is much likelier than the American Department of Justice (DoJ) to fear that a merger of two big firms or the behaviour of a dominant one will force rivals out of business, raising prices and restricting choice. The Americans are more confident that if powerful firms abuse their strength, they may attract competition rather than crush it.

American regulators seem to have become more convinced of this argument than their European counterparts have. The saga of Microsoft illustrates the difference. In 1998 the DoJ charged that by bundling Internet Explorer, its web browser, with Windows, its operating system, Microsoft sought to extend its desktop monopoly into browsers, freezing out Netscape, its main competitor.

The American courts ruled against Microsoft and in April 2000 ordered that the software giant should be split into two— one part owning the operating system and the other owning all other applications. The next year an appeals court said that Microsoft's actions did not warrant dismemberment. The DoJ settled for far more lenient remedies. These would stop Microsoft from bullying PC manufacturers into favouring its add-ons to Windows, but would leave the firm and its most important product intact.

The difference in approach is partly explained by economic philosophy. In America there is a greater faith that markets will fix the problem of monopolies and a belief that market leadership in high-tech is transient. A new product may make today's dominant technology redundant tomorrow. Firms compete for the market as much as in it: temporary monopoly is the reward for innovation.

But in a market where one firm is king, such practices can take on a sinister guise. Dominant firms might use loyalty rebates to stop others from becoming large enough to pose a serious threat. Bundling can be a tactic to compel consumers to buy several things from a firm with a monopoly in one product. It is hard to establish whether such strategies are pro-competitive or nefarious. Antitrust watchdogs have to gauge the tangible short-term benefits of lower prices and convenience against theoretical long-term harm.

America's agencies have tended to judge that too little action is less of a risk than too much. Intervention to protect weaker firms may serve only to blunt competition for the sake of highly uncertain benefits. Andrew Dick, a former DoJ economist now at CRA International, a consultancy, says that for these reasons American competition authorities put their faith in entrepreneurship to tackle monopolies. "Someone will always come along and build a better mousetrap," he says.

—The Economist **(May 1, 2008)**

Questions

1. Be prepared to discuss in class the concept of monopoly as a "restraint of trade" in the market for computer software.
2. Take a position favoring the European Commission's view of mergers or that of the Department of Justice, and be prepared to defend your position with facts, analysis, and arguments from this article and other readings.

2. What Are the Consequences of Expanding Demand in the Global Micro Market for Crude Oil?

Our discussion of the American equities markets can be a starting point for a discussion of the energy markets in general and the market for petroleum or crude oil in particular. In 2009, the world was consuming approximately 86 million barrels of crude oil every day. Of that total, the United States was consuming approximately 19 million barrels, of which it was producing 7 million barrels and importing almost 12 million barrels. Just as there are different stocks in the equities markets, there are different types of crude oil, "West Texas Sweet," "Brent," "Siberian Blend," and "North forties" among others. The following article discusses some of the forces of supply and demand that bear upon the markets for crude oil.

Oil Market Remains Vulnerable

LONDON—Though demand for fuels is eroding fast, especially in the U.S., the global oil market remains tight, susceptible to sudden external shocks able to arrest the recent downdraft in prices.

One such disruption—a fire on a critical pipeline through Turkey—is imperiling the flow of Caspian oil to global markets.

The explosion on the Baku-Tbilisi-Ceyhan, or BTC, pipeline helped drive U.S. crude prices up, reversing a four-week slide. In midday trading Thursday on the New York Mercantile Exchange, crude for September delivery was up $1.22 a barrel at $119.80.

Events in Turkey came against a backdrop of bearish signals, with oil imports to the U.S. rising and evidence that an economic slowdown was eating away at demand. The latest data from the U.S. Department of Energy, released Wednesday, showed crude inventories building much more than expected, though they still are below the five-year average.

But supply concerns weigh heavily on the market. Militant attacks on oil infrastructure in Nigeria continue, and there are still fears of a showdown over Iran's nuclear ambitions, which could halt oil exports out of the Gulf. Oil production outside the Middle East continues to disappoint as major projects are hit by fresh delays.

The fire at BTC, by far the worst incident to affect the one million barrels-a-day pipeline since it was commissioned in 2005, broke out early Wednesday and continues to rage. Rebels from the Kurdistan Workers' Party, or PKK, claimed responsibility for the blast that caused the fire in a statement on their Web site.

But a spokesman for the pipeline's operator, Botas International Ltd., said the cause, whether sabotage or a technical fault, was unclear. He said he expected the fire to burn itself out within a couple of days, but it was too early to say how long the pipeline would be out of action.

Oil from the BTC line is an important source of the 86 million barrels consumed globally each day.

Any sustained outage would have a big impact on Azerbaijan, one of the biggest oil producers in the region, which sends most of its exports through the BTC. BP PLC, of the U.K., which is a BTC shareholder, said it is being forced to curtail production at two big oil and natural-gas fields it operates in the Caspian Sea to avoid a buildup of crude at its onshore facilities. On Wednesday it declared force majeure on exports, meaning it may not be able to fulfill contractual obligations.

Running for more than 1,600 kilometers through Azerbaijan, Georgia and Turkey, BTC is one of the most strategically important pieces of energy infrastructure in the world. Strongly backed by the U.S., it was designed to be the first major pipeline to bring

Caspian oil to Western markets without going through Russia, and thereby to ease Moscow's tight grip on oil exports from the region.

A spokeswoman for BP in Azerbaijan's capital, Baku, said the company was cutting back on production at Azeri-Chirag-Gunashli, or ACG, a complex of oil fields about 120 kilometers off the Azeri coast that produce some 800,000 barrels of crude a day, and at Shah Deniz, a big natural-gas reservoir that also yields some liquid condensates. She declined to say how much production would be closed.

The "precautionary measure" would help BP manage stock levels at the oil terminal near Baku that supplies BTC, she said. BP also is considering increased use of alternative export routes. These include a rail link to the Georgian Black Sea port of Batumi, a pipeline to Supsa, also in Georgia, and another pipeline to Novorossiisk, a Russian port on the Black Sea.

But the total combined capacity of the two alternative pipelines is 200,000 barrels a day—a fifth of BTC's capacity. The Baku-Novorossiisk pipeline is also unpopular because oil transported through it is blended during transit with lower-quality Russian crude. The resulting mix trades at a discount to the industry benchmark Brent, though the Russian pipeline monopoly Transneft pays no compensation for the loss in value, according to consultancy Wood Mackenzie.

—**Guy Chazan,** **Wall Street Journal** (August 8, 2008)

Questions

1. Be prepared to discuss in class the factors that bear upon the market price of crude oil as it moves from the production fields to the consumer in the form of home heating oil or gasoline for automobile travel.
2. With your fellow students, role-play a meeting of the Organization of Petroleum Exporting Countries (OPEC) and consider the following factors, as well as other sources of information, while formulating your recommendation for action by the OPEC Production Council.
   - OPEC members control approximately 80 percent of the world's "proven" petroleum reserves.
   - OPEC's petroleum production constitutes approximately 40 percent of the world's production of crude oil.
   - OPEC relies on production controls (supply) to effect changes in the price of crude oil in the world's petroleum markets.
   - Approximately half of OPEC members are concerned with optimizing their revenues, and the other half with "price stability."

REVIEW QUESTIONS

1. What did Adam Smith refer to by using the term "invisible hand of the market"?
   a. That consumers and producers naturally find each other for transactions to happen in an unregulated market.
   b. That free markets and competition can lead to socially desirable results (to optimality in production and consumption).
   c. That a free market has self-regulation properties and no government intervention is therefore needed.
   d. That a free market leads producers to produce in the correct quantities.
2. Which of the following terms refers to the facilities offered to market participants and rules and regulations that govern trading?
   a. Market microstructure.
   b. Market architecture.
   c. Market efficiency.
   d. Micro market.
3. Which of the following statements about fixed and variable costs is FALSE?
   a. All costs are variable in the long run.
   b. Marginal analysis cannot be applied to fixed costs.
   c. Fixed costs are relevant for the decision making process.
   d. Variable costs are relevant for the decision making process.
4. Elasticity
   a. Is measured is percentage terms.
   b. Is a percentage change in dependent variable (quantity) divided by the percentage change in independent variable (price).
   c. Cannot be a negative number.
   d. Is a measure of responsiveness of an independent variable (price) to a dependent variable (quantity).
5. What does "*ceteris paribus*" mean?
   a. "In a dynamic environment."
   b. "Ignoring market frictions."
   c. "Given that market is competitive."
   d. "All else being equal."
6. The market where newly issued shares of stock are traded is referred to as a
   a. Secondary market.
   b. Dealer market.
   c. Primary market.
   d. De-novo market.

7. Which of the following statements about trading and investing is correct?
   a. Trading is the implementation of investment decisions.
   b. Investing is the implementation of trading decisions.
   c. Trading and investing are identical concepts.
   d. None of the above is correct.

8. Which of the following is NOT a reason why market(s) may operate imperfectly?
   a. Public goods.
   b. Trading costs.
   c. Imperfect information.
   d. Rational behavior.

9. Which of the following terms refers to a contrast of the two different static equilibria that is attributable to a difference in the value of an independent variable?
   a. Market microstructure.
   b. Differential equilibria.
   c. Comparative statics.
   d. Smithsonian equilibria.

10. Which of the following statements about the adjustment process in the short run and in the long run is correct?
    a. Decision makers' responses to the changes in economic variables do not occur instantaneously, and for that reason we differentiate between the short run and the long run.
    b. The length of the "long run" is taken to be 3 to 10 years for the majority of the micro markets.
    c. Short-run adjustments are more complete than the long-run adjustments.
    d. Both a and b are correct.

11. A micro market that makes it possible for its participants to trade "reasonably quickly, in reasonable amounts, and at reasonable prices" is referred to as
    a. Competitive.
    b. Liquid.
    c. Reasonable.
    d. Balanced.

12. The study of operations of the equity markets is called
    a. Micro market economics.
    b. Equity market architecture.
    c. Equity market microstructure.
    d. Equity microeconomics.

13. The price of coffee went up by 20¢ from its previous level at $2.00 and your demand for coffee went down from 10 cups a week to 9 cups. What is your elasticity of demand for coffee?
    a. −1.
    b. −5.
    c. 1.
    d. 5.
14. When there is only one firm selling a certain good in the marketplace, that firm is a
    a. Monopsonist.
    b. Monopolist.
    c. Price taker.
    d. Dealer.
15. Which of the following represents a classic (i.e., a conventional) set of factors of production?
    a. Land, labor, physical capital, and financial capital.
    b. Land, labor, physical capital, and human capital.
    c. Land, labor, physical capital, and information.
    d. None of the above.

APPLICATIONS AND ISSUES

1. **Why was the New York Stock Exchange founded?**
   During the first year of the federal government and the presidency of George Washington, Congress accepted the plan of Secretary of the Treasury Alexander Hamilton to refinance the Revolutionary War debt that accumulated while winning independence from the British. To fund this refinancing, the federal government sold bonds to various investors in what we might now call an initial public offering (IPO). Subsequently, those investors wished to buy or sell those federal government bonds. The brokers who traded those bonds gathered daily under a buttonwood tree on Wall Street to meet with the investors and to trade the government's "stock." Thus the "Buttonwood Agreement" was formed and the New York Stock Exchange was founded.
   Common equity stock of industrial enterprises did not become widely owned and traded investments until the last years of the nineteenth century when investment banker J. P. Morgan and his firm brought the equity shares of many large companies to be traded on the floor of the NYSE.

2. **Symmetric information, imperfect information, and the "lemon" problem**

Market imperfections have often been recognized as imperfect competition and illustrated by the differing bodies of knowledge possessed by buyers and sellers in a micro market. For example, the seller of a good usually has been its owner and therefore is very familiar with its attributes, including its imperfections. It follows logically that a primary motive in selling a good is dissatisfaction with the good's imperfections. Therefore, the owner knows he owns a "lemon" and wishes to sell (unload) it. Conversely, the buyer has no such knowledge of the good's imperfections and therefore is at a disadvantage when compared to the knowledge possessed by the seller. Does this "Lemon" problem suggest that markets can never be fair because of asymmetric information? Those who complain of market failures and "imperfect competition" cite this phenomenon as a reason for inherent market failure. What is your view?

3. **Elasticities of supply and demand**

The supply of goods coming into the markets is determined by several different forces. Similarly, the demand for goods in the market is affected by a variety of forces bearing on buyers. As we have noted, the primary determinant of both supply and demand are the prices for the goods in the market. As prices increase, the demand by consumers for that good falls. Conversely, when the price of a good rises, the producers of that good see an increasingly lucrative profit opportunity and will therefore seek to increase production (that is, increase the quantity supplied of that good). So price would seem to be the primary determinant of quantity demanded and quantity supplied, as well as of the supply and demand.

Yet we need to go deeper into the consumer's and the producer's decision to produce or consume a good. For example, it seems logical that the consumer's willingness to consume is determined by the amount of income that the consumer possesses. More income generally leads to more consumption. We can then suggest that the higher the income the higher will be the propensity to consume. Therefore consumption is not only price elastic, it is also "income elastic." Surely, there are other attributes of the consumer that will bear on consumption, and the demand for a good will have many elasticities (one for each attribute).

On the supply side the same concept of elasticities holds true. Supply is price elastic, but it also responds to costs of production, so we know that production is "cost elastic." Finally, we know that the demand and supply for goods responds to the prices of related goods.

When the price of gas goes up, the demand for cars goes down. We call this "cross price elasticity." We treat this in more detail in Chapter 3.

4. **The market for gasoline and the alternatives of a "market-based" solution contrasted with government-directed "solutions"**

   To spark debate and discussion, some members of the class should be assigned to be advocates for "alternative fuels" and their promotion by market action or by government sponsorship.

ADDITIONAL READINGS

Heilbronner, Robert L., and William Milberg. *The Making of Economic Society*. Upper Saddle River, NJ: Prentice-Hall, 2002.

   A survey of the evolution of price-driven markets and their role in enhancing economic growth.

Hyne, Paul, Peter J. Boettke, and David L. Prychitko. *The Economic Way of Thinking*. Upper Saddle River, NJ: Pearson/Prentice-Hall, 2006.

   A useful reference restatement of classical microeconomics for amplification.

Schwartz, Robert A., Reto Francioni, and Bruce Weber. *The Equity Trader Course*. Hoboken, NJ: John Wiley & Sons, 2004.

   A definitive advanced text for equity market professional traders.

Sharp, Ansel M., Charles Register, and Paul Grimes. *Economics of Social Issues*. New York: McGraw-Hill, 2006.

   A reference guide to the definitions of normative economic problems as evolving from market pricing.

ANSWERS TO REVIEW QUESTIONS

1. b
2. b
3. c
4. b
5. d
6. c
7. a
8. d
9. c
10. a
11. b
12. c
13. a
14. b
15. d

CHAPTER 2

The Consumer Choice Model

What Would You Really Like to Do?

LEARNING OBJECTIVES

- **Recognize how a budget constraint delineates the choices available to a consumer.** An individual consumer is always constrained by the scarcity of resources. Because resources can be used to fulfill different needs in different ways, trade-offs exist (that is, there are opportunities to substitute one scarce economic resource for another). The budget constraint for a consumer divides alternative consumption bundles that are obtainable from alternative bundles that are not obtainable, given the consumer's income or wealth and the structure of relative prices.

- **Understand how an indifference curve mapping describes a consumer's preferences.** An indifference curve mapping describes a consumer's tastes (or preferences) for various economic resources. This chapter simplifies the picture by dealing with only two resources. The two-dimensional indifference curve mapping reflects the ease with which the consumer would be willing to substitute one of the two economic resources for the other. Interfacing the family of indifference curves with a budget constraint identifies the optimal (utility maximizing) consumption combination for the consumer. The chapter explains all of this with reference to three different trade-offs: X versus Y, present consumption versus future consumption, and the risk and return characteristics of a risky financial asset.

- **Understand the meanings of risk and return, and a risk-return trade-off.** It is important to understand exactly what *risk-aversion* means and why we assume that decision makers are risk-averse. Different individuals have varying tolerances for risk. Those with a low risk tolerance require

17

a high reward (a high expected return) for bearing risk. You should appreciate how our indifference curve, budget constraint analysis can be used to resolve the risk and return trade-off for a risk-averse decision maker.

■ **You should begin to be able to formalize a consumer's response to changes in prices and/or his or her income.** When relative prices change and/or income or wealth changes, the budget constraint shifts and there are changes to the optimal utility-maximizing basket. Start thinking about how a decision maker's response to a budget constraint shift depends on his or her willingness to substitute one consumption bundle for another. Further recognize that the willingness to substitute is reflected in the shapes of the decision maker's indifference curves.

■ **Understand the difference between positive economics and normative economics.** You will hopefully be able to use the terms appropriately: Positive economics is all about *predicting* what will happen in response to an economic variable changing. Normative economics is a matter of saying, not what the response will be, but what it *should* be

■ **Be able to decompose the impact of a price change into an income effect and a substitution effect.** Income constant, a price increase for any one good reduces the ability of a decision maker to acquire all other goods/ services. Conversely, a price reduction for any one good increases a decision maker's command over all goods/services. Thus you should understand that a price change not only results in one resource becoming more or less expensive *relative to* other resources, but that it also changes *real* (as distinct from nominal) income. Thus the response to a price change can be decomposed into two effects: an income effect (the "pure" response to a change in income) and a substitution effect (the "pure" response to a change in relative prices).

■ **Be able to apply the consumer choice model to three decisions a household might make.** The chapters discusses in detail the choices concerning generic goods X and Y, concerning current and future consumption, and concerning the risk and return characteristics of a financial portfolio.

■ **Gain familiarity with the Capital Asset Pricing Model.** CAPM is an important cornerstone of modern portfolio theory. It is also an excellent example of how the indifference-curve, budget-constraint model of consumer choice that we have been dealing with (itself a cornerstone of microeconomic theory) can be applied to a trade-off that is of central importance to all of us: the trade-off between risk and return.

CHAPTER SUMMARY

The chapter presents the consumer choice model with regard to three different trade-offs, which each involve two items: (1) a trade-off between generic good or service X and generic good or service Y, (2) a current consumption versus future consumption trade-off, and (3) the risk, return trade-off that plays a central role in modern portfolio theory. As you will appreciate when we get to Chapter 3, with the consumer choice model in hand we can derive a decision maker's demand curve for a good or service, or for a financial asset.

Various key thoughts were developed in the chapter that you should have a solid grasp of the following nine points:

1. To resolve optimally the two-item trade-offs, two relationships were specified for each trade-off: (1) a budget constraint that demarks the "obtainable set" (the alternative achievable combinations of the two items), and (2) a family of indifference curves that can be derived from the decision maker's utility function, which describes his or her tastes.

2. When the decision maker has resolved the trade-offs optimally (that is, has selected a combination that maximizes his or her utility or expected utility), his or her tastes are harmonized (on the margin) with the realities of the marketplace. Specifically, when the decision maker has achieved an optimal combination of the two factors, the ratio of relative prices (as given by the slope of the budget constraint) equals the ratio of marginal utilities (as given by the slope of the highest indifference curve that he or she can reach).

3. For the X, Y trade-off and the present consumption, future consumption trade-off, both items are "a good" and the decision maker's indifference mappings for these goods are negatively inclined. For the risk-return trade-off, expected return is "a good"—the decision maker's expected utility is higher when the expected return is higher (risk constant), but risk is "a bad"—the decision maker's expected utility is lower when the risk is higher (expected return constant). This is because the decision maker is assumed to have a risk-averse utility function for income (or wealth). With return a good and risk a bad, risk-return indifference curves are positively inclined.

4. The decision maker's risk aversion is not attributable to any attitude regarding the act of risk-taking per se (i.e., the fun or displeasure that might be derived from playing a risky game), but to the decision maker's utility of wealth increasing at a diminishing rate. Consider a betting situation that is fair in monetary terms. A bet is fair if the expected net monetary payout from taking the bet is zero. With the utility of income (or of wealth) decreasing on the margin, the utility gained from winning

a bet that is fair in monetary terms is less than the utility that is lost when the fair bet is lost.

5. That is, if a bet offers you an equal chance of winning or of losing a dollar, the utility you would gain from the dollar you might win is less (remember, your marginal utility of dollars is decreasing) than the utility you would lose by losing a dollar. Thus, your expected utility gain from taking the bet is negative. Consequently, in utility terms the bet is not fair, which means that a positive expected monetary return must be offered if a risk-averse participant is to accept taking the risk.

6. To analyze a risk-return trade-off for an investor, a stock's (or portfolio's) expected return was given precise definition. Strictly speaking, it is the expected logarithm of price relatives, with prices having been adjusted for cash and stock dividends, and for stock splits. Risk was defined as the variance of logarithmic returns, assuming that returns are lognormally distributed. For simplicity, however, we suppressed the label "logarithm" and dealt with arithmetic returns as if they are normally distributed.

7. In point 4, we have noted that a risk-averse investor will accept a risky situation only if compensated for taking the risk. The compensation is in the form of a higher expected return, and the amount of compensation that is required to induce the investor to take the risk is a "risk premium."

8. With the four key terms identified (risk-aversion, expected return, risk, and risk premium), the risk-return trade-off was analyzed assuming two financial assets: (1) a risky market portfolio (e.g., a well-diversified mutual fund) and (2) a risk-free asset (e.g., Treasury bills). Working in this setting we obtained (1) a budget constraint that we called the "Capital Market Line" and (2) a family of positively inclined risk, return indifference curves. These curves, and the optimality solution that they delivered, are consistent with the Capital Asset Pricing Model (CAPM), a cornerstone of modern portfolio theory.

9. The preceding equilibrium models were extended to show how the optimal selection of a factor (the generic good X, current consumption, or the acceptance of risk) changes when the price of the factor changes, all other independent variables being constant. These comparative static results are generalized in Chapter 3 to give us the decision maker's demand curve for each of the factors.

GLOSSARY

budget constraint The constraint that identifies the alternative combinations of goods and services that a decision maker can obtain, given prices, and the decision maker's income (M). In a two-good model (X and Y), the constraint is the linear equation,

$$Y = \frac{M}{P_Y} - \left(\frac{P_X}{P_Y}\right) X$$

capital (types of) Physical capital (such as plant and equipment), human capital (such as education and health), financial capital (such as equities, bonds, and derivatives), and goodwill.

Capital Asset Pricing Model (CAPM) A cornerstone of modern portfolio theory that shows how risk and expected return are related in the market, and how individual stocks are priced given their systematic risk (their covariance with the market portfolio).

capital market line An upward sloping line that delineates the risk-return trade-off that investors face in a CAPM framework when combining shares of a market portfolio with a risk-free asset. The capital market line plays the same role with respect to the risk-return trade-off as the standard budget constraint plays with respect to the generic X, Y trade-off.

comparative statics A contrast of different equilibria for a dependent variable for different values of an independent variable, all else constant.

expected return The return that a risky stock or stock portfolio is expected to yield as of a period of time that has not ended yet. If returns are (lognormally) distributed, the expected return is the mean of the lognormal distribution.

expected utility The utility that a decision maker expects to achieve from acquiring a risky position.

factors of production An element (but not an ingredient, as flour is for cake) in production for which there is supply, demand, and a market-determined price. Productive factors are traditionally classified as land, labor, and capital, as identified by Adam Smith. We have also included information and financial capital as factors of production. Closely associated with financial capital is liquidity, a more encompassing but more abstract concept.

fair bet A risk situation with an expected monetary return of zero.

fixed costs costs of production that do not vary with output. Fixed costs exist in the short run. In the long run all costs are variable.

flow variable A variable that is measured as a rate per unit of time (in contrast with a stock-dimensioned variable that is measured as of a point in time). For instance, the amount of a resource consumed (or output produced) during an hour, a day, a month, or a year. Income, consumption, and stock returns are examples of flow-dimensioned variables.

indifference curve In a two-good environment (X and Y), the locus of all combinations of X and Y that yield the same total utility. If constrained to a single indifference curve, the decision maker is indifferent about the specific point on the curve that he or she is at. Indifference curves for a utility mapping are analogous to the contour lines of a topographical map.

marginal rate of substitution In a two-good model (X and Y), the slope of an indifference curve as given by the negative of the ratio of the marginal utility of X to the marginal utility of Y. The ratio of marginal utilities is the rate at which a consumer would be willing to trade one good for another while neither augmenting nor diminishing his or her utility.

price taker   A market participant who, being of insignificant size in the market, has no power to affect the price that is set in the marketplace. Having no power over price, such a participant may be referred to as being "atomistic."

risk and return trade-off   When return has been maximized for a given level of risk, and risk has been minimized for a given level of return, the amount of additional risk that has to be accepted in order to achieve a higher expected return or, alternatively viewed, the lower expected return that has to be accepted in order to achieve a lower level of risk.

risk and uncertainty   In a risk situation, the distribution of possible outcomes and their associated probabilities are known. With risk, the parameters of a distribution (such as its mean and variance) are known. Under uncertainty, the distribution of outcomes and their associated probabilities are not known. Uncertainty can in principle be reduced by information collection; risk cannot be reduced by gathering more information per se, but it can be controlled by appropriate hedging and portfolio formation.

risk premium   The positive difference between the expected return for a risk position and a risk-free return that is required to induce an investor to accept taking the risky position.

standard deviation   A measure of dispersion that is applied to distributions. The square root of variance.

stock variable   A variable that is measured as of a point in time (in contrast with a flow variable, which is measured as a rate per unit of time). Wealth, an inventory position, and a stock price are examples of a stock-dimensioned variable.

variable costs   Costs of producing a good that vary with the amount of the good produced. In the long run, all costs are variable.

CURRENT EVENTS DISCUSSIONS

1. Since Products Appear in Different Markets in Different Forms, Can They Be Said to Be Interdependent?

The microstructures of many different markets respond to the utility and risk parameters that we have discussed using the equity markets as our model. In recognizing the measurement of these parameters, we should not lose sight that these market microstructures operate in a similar fashion in most markets. The following discussion of U.S. consumption of petroleum products over the past 30 years illustrates this similarity. The many distinctive variants of crude oil—West Texas Sweet, Brent (North Sea), and Brunei—all have their own micro markets. More importantly for consumers, products manufactured from crude oil—gasoline, jet fuel, diesel fuel, asphalt, and electricity—also have their micro markets where the utility and risk appetites of consumers are encountered.

A Difficult Road Awaits for Energy Conservation

Soaring gasoline prices, angst in Washington, economic malaise, fears of far worse to come—the U.S. has been through the energy wringer before, and even managed to ease the pain through conservation.

The last time the country was clobbered, 1979–1983, Americans cut way back on driving, bought far fewer and smaller cars and dramatically reduced the use of oil. It's natural to assume that we can do it again.

But conserving our way out of this crunch won't be so easy. Here are five key reasons why.

1. The easy stuff is done

The cuts in oil use made between 1979 and 1983 look impressive. In four years, the country weaned itself off of 3.3 million barrels a day, a drop of nearly 20%. Not until 1997 did the U.S. get back to the same level of oil consumption it had in 1979.

But half of that cut, in residual fuel oil for electricity generation, was relatively painless and can't be repeated. The U. S. by 1983 had slashed consumption by 1.4 million barrels of oil a day by switching power stations over to coal or natural gas. Today, the country consumes fewer than 700,000 barrels of residual fuel a day, almost entirely in ships. So any similar cuts this time will have to come on America's highways, not in its power plants.

2. We're bigger, busier, and wealthier now

Americans in 1979 embarked on a forced conservation kick unrivaled since World War II. By 1983, gasoline use had fallen almost 11%.

Today, the U.S. is a vastly more fuel-thirsty place. Yes, gasoline use is tapering off. But in April of this year, the U.S. consumed 9.1 million barrels of gasoline a day, two million more than in April 1979—partly because Americans are now driving almost twice as many miles a day as they did then.

Meanwhile, the economy is also nearly five times as large, so the impact of record-high fuel prices is still more muted.

3. **And yet, globally, the U.S. matters less**

   In 1979, of every 100 barrels of oil produced globally, 29 went into American cars, trucks, planes, ships, homes and power plants. Today, that figure has fallen to less than 24 of every 100 barrels. U.S. consumption has grown, but global use has grown much more—and there's the rub.

   Slashed demand in industrialized countries in the early 1980s came straight off the oil ledger, because that's where most of the demand was. Nearly half of the drop came from the U.S. alone.

   This year, growth elsewhere will far outpace slumping demand in almost every Western developed country. In all, global demand is expected to rise by about one million barrels a day, despite the historic run-up in prices. It's what happens in China now that really counts.

4. **This time, it's supply *and* demand**

   The 1979 energy crisis was all about supply. Turmoil in the Middle East took millions of barrels off the market, so prices soared. But just as prices peaked, in the spring of 1981, huge new stashes of oil were coming onstream in Mexico, the North Sea and Alaska. Soon enough, the world was again awash in oil.

   Today's forces are far more complex, and gloomier. Booming demand in the Middle East and Asia is colliding with rising fears of a long-term supply pinch. Unlike in 1979, there is no North Sea about to open up, while the Saudis are pumping almost full out.

5. **Recessions help**

   Getting whacked by gasoline prices prodded Americans to cut back in the early 1980s, but so did joblessness, stagflation and a horrible economy. Unemployment topped 7%, while mortgage rates hovered in the teens. Gasoline use and car sales plunged partly because people were working less for a dollar that also bought less. Economists note that nothing whittles down energy use quite as effectively as a recession. Today's less sluggish economy is less likely to force our hand on conservation.

   On the bright side, efficiencies gained now appear much likelier to last. After the last shock, oil became abundant again, prices plummeted and Detroit found clever ways to bypass fuel-efficiency standards to give Americans the huge sport-utility vehicles they wanted. Now, car companies are scrambling to churn out a new generation of smaller, more efficient vehicles and investing in fuel-saving technology that was viewed as too expensive to bother with when oil was cheap.

—*Wall Street Journal* (July 22, 2008)

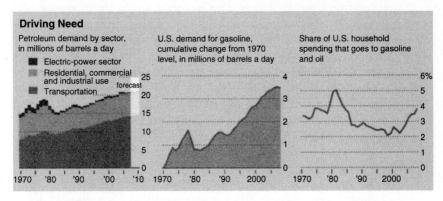

Driving Need

Petroleum demand by sector, in millions of barrels a day
- Electric-power sector
- Residential, commercial and industrial use
- Transportation

U.S. demand for gasoline, cumulative change from 1970 level, in millions of barrels a day

Share of U.S. household spending that goes to gasoline and oil

Source: U.S. Energy Information Administration; Commerce Department via Cambridge Economic Research Associates.

Questions

1. For a class discussion on the prospects of "sustainable" development of alternative sources of energy, be prepared to present your recommendations for substantial reductions in American petroleum consumption.
2. The factors below bear upon the consideration of nuclear energy as a substitute for coal and petroleum in the production of electric power in the United States.
   - Currently electricity is produced from the following sources.
     1. Coal—51 percent
     2. Natural Gas—21 percent
     3. Nuclear—19 percent
     4. Hydro and "renewable"—5 percent
     5. Petroleum—4 percent
   - Considering market demand and the above supply factors, take a position regarding the use of nuclear energy for the production of electricity in the United States.

2. Does Government Direct or Influence Consumer Choice?

The Consumer Choice model and the concept of the risk-reward trade-off have moved from our realm of microeconomic analysis to that of taxation and trade. As much as the two consumers, Harrison and Alba, might consider the advantages of current consumption compared to future consumption, they wish to be *compensated for their deferral of current consumption*. Further, as they seek to optimize their future consumption by deferring current consumption through saving, they expect a return from anyone who wishes to use their deferred consumption, their savings. As they are willing to accept a certain probability of loss, they are not entirely averse to taking a risk. Yet they also insist upon being compensated with a *risk premium* for bearing that risk The use of these concepts of the Consumer Choice model are now being considered in the formation of government tax policy. The discussion below between two prominent economists gives some of the reasons and consequences for the use of the Consumer Choice concepts.

Dynamic Analysis

By Robert Carroll and N. Gregory Mankiw

Does tax relief mean more economic growth? Many people believe the answer is yes, and now they get strong support from the staff of the U.S. Treasury.

Most press reports on the Mid-Session Review of the federal budget, released by the Bush administration a couple of weeks ago, focused on the good news about expanding tax revenues and the shrinking budget deficit. But for tax-policy geeks, the most intriguing part of the report was an easily overlooked box on page 3: "A Dynamic Analysis of Permanent Extension of the President's Tax Relief." Over the past six months, the Treasury Department staff has been studying the dynamic effects of tax cuts on the economy. The results of this analysis, previewed in this box, were released yesterday in more complete form (available at http://www.treas. gov/offices/tax-policy/).

A bit of background: Most official analysis of tax policy is based on what economists call "static assumptions." While many microeconomic behavioral responses are included, the future path of macroeconomic variables such as the capital stock and GNP are assumed to stay the same, regardless of tax policy. This approach is not realistic, but it has been the tradition in tax analysis mainly because it is simple and convenient.

In his 2007 budget, President Bush directed the Treasury staff to develop a dynamic analysis of tax policy, and we are now reaping the fruits of those efforts. The staff uses a model that does not consider the short-run effects of tax policy on the business cycle, but instead focuses on its longer-run effects on economic growth through the incentives to work, save, and invest, and to allocate capital among competing uses.

The Treasury report describes what will happen to the economy if the tax relief of the past few years is made permanent, compared to the alternative scenario of reverting back to the tax code as it was in 2000. Specifically, the report analyzes the effects of lower taxes on dividends and capital gains, the effects of lower taxes on ordinary income, and the extension of other tax cuts, including the new 10 percent bracket, the expanded child credit and marriage-penalty relief. Here are three main lessons.

Lesson No. 1: Lower tax rates lead to a more prosperous economy.

According to the Treasury analysis, a permanent extension of the recent tax cuts leads to a long-run increase in the capital stock of 2.3%, and a long-run increase in GNP of 0.7%. In today's economy, such a GNP expansion would mean an extra $90 billion a year that the nation can spend on consumer goods to raise living standards, or capital goods to maintain prosperity. More than two-thirds of this expansion occurs within 10 years.

Lesson No. 2: Not all taxes are created equal for purposes of promoting growth.

Some tax rate reductions have a profound impact on incentives and economic growth, while others have minimal or even adverse effects. The Treasury staff reports particularly large bang-for-the-buck from the reductions in dividends and capital-gains taxes. Even though these tax cuts account for less than 20% of the static revenue loss from permanent tax relief, they produce more than half of the long-run growth.

At the opposite end of the spectrum are the tax reductions from the 10% bracket, child credit and marriage-penalty relief. These tax cuts put money in people's pockets when, during the recent recession, the economy needed a short-run boost to aggregate demand. They also fulfill other objectives, such as making the tax system more progressive. But they illustrate that not all tax cuts promote long-run growth. Treasury estimates that without the tax reductions from the 10% bracket, child credit and marriage-penalty relief, the long-run increase in GNP would be larger—1.1% rather than 0.7%.

Lesson No. 3: How tax relief is financed is crucial for its economic impact.

Like all of us, the government eventually has to pay its bills. In technical terms, the government faces an inter-temporal budget constraint that ties the present value of government spending to the present value of tax revenue. This means that when taxes are cut, other offsetting adjustments are required to make the numbers add up.

The Treasury's main analysis assumes that lower tax revenue will over time be accompanied by reduced spending on government consumption. But the report also shows what happens if spending cuts are not forthcoming. In this alternative scenario, a permanent extension of recent tax relief is assumed to lead to an eventual increase in income taxes.

The results are strikingly different. Instead of increasing by 0.7% in the long run, GNP now falls by 0.9%. Tax relief is good for growth, but only if the tax reductions are financed by spending restraint. One exception: Lower taxes on dividends and capital gains promote growth, even if they require higher income taxes.

These Treasury results are sure to spark debate and further research. While the Treasury report is not the last word on dynamic analysis, it is a big step toward a more realistic view of tax policy.

—Wall Street Journal **(July 28, 2006)**

Questions

1. Given the progress of personal consumption expenditures, be prepared to discuss in class your concurrence or dissent from the above "Lessons."
2. The president has called the cabinet into special executive session. As a highly regarded microstructure-oriented economist and the replacement for the current secretary of the treasury, what market-oriented recommendations would you provide the president?

REVIEW QUESTIONS

1. The slope of a budget constraint in a consumer choice model is
   a. The price relative, P_X/P_Y.
   b. The price relative, P_Y/P_X.
   c. The negative of the price relative, $-(P_X/P_Y)$.
   d. The negative of the price relative, $-(P_Y/P_X)$.
2. The consumer choice model in the absence of risk and uncertainty has a goal of
   a. Maximizing expected utility.
   b. Maximizing the total unit consumption of both goods.

    c. Minimizing the cost of a target basket of goods.

    d. None of the above.

3. Which of the following is correct about stock-dimensioned and flow-dimensioned variables?

    a. Variables expressed as rates per unit of time are flow-dimensioned.

    b. Variables measured at a specific point in time are stock-dimensioned.

    c. Both a and b are correct.

    d. None of the above is correct.

4. Which of the following statements about the budget constraint and the indifference curves in a consumer choice model is correct?

    a. The slope of an indifference curve defines the rate at which an individual would be willing to exchange good X for good Y while keeping his/her utility level unchanged.

    b. The slope of a budget constraint defines a relative price of two goods, that is, the rate at which good X and good Y can be exchanged in the marketplace.

    c. The point of tangency between the budget constraint and the utility curve defines the specific combination of good X and good Y that aligns an individual's preferences with the market prices.

    d. All of the above are correct.

5. In the context of a current consumption, future consumption model, reducing your consumption at $t = 1$ by \$1 would result in

    a. Reducing your consumption at $t = 0$ by $(1 + r)$ dollars.

    b. Increasing your consumption at $t = 0$ by $(1 + r)$ dollars.

    c. Reducing your consumption at $t = 0$ by $1/(1 + r)$ dollars.

    d. Increasing your consumption at $t = 0$ by $1/(1 + r)$ dollars.

       To answer questions 6 through 7, use the current consumption, future consumption model. Assume that your income is \$50,000 in year 0 and \$55,000 in year 1, and that the annual interest rate is 10 percent.

6. What are the price relative (relative price of current consumption to future consumption) and the slope of the budget constraint?

    a. 0.9 and −0.9.

    b. 1.1 and −1.1.

    c. 1 and 0.9.

    d. 0.1 and −0.9.

7. What is your maximum attainable consumption in year 0 and in year 1?

    a. \$100,000; \$110,000.

    b. \$110,000; \$100,000.

    c. \$50,000; \$55,500.

    d. \$55,500; \$50,000.

8. Which of the following statements about risk and uncertainty is FALSE?

a. The term *risk* applies when the full range of outcomes is identifiable and a probability number can be assigned to each of the possible outcomes.

b. The term *uncertainty* applies when you do not know either the full range of outcomes, or their associated probabilities, or both.

c. Uncertainty can typically be diminished (though not necessarily eliminated) by gathering more information.

d. Uncertainty can be controlled by proper diversification, portfolio balancing, and otherwise hedging risk positions (e.g., with financial derivatives).

Use the following scenario to answer questions 9 through 10. You are asked to pay $10 to play a fair coin-flip game. If it is heads, you get $20, and if it is tails, you get nothing.

9. If you refuse to play this game, you can be characterized as (a)
   a. Risk seeker.
   b. Risk averse.
   c. Risk neutral.
   d. Risk negative.

10. If you refuse to play this game but would agree to play if you were offered $25 or more (instead of $20), if it is heads, then your risk premium in dollars and as a percent is
    a. 2.5; 10 percent.
    b. 2.5; 25 percent.
    c. 5; 50 percent.
    d. None of the above.

11. If you drive on a three-lane highway (in each direction), and you have no idea whether the exit that is coming up in half a mile will be to the left or to the right, but you select a right-hand lane, you are
    a. Risk neutral.
    b. Risk averse.
    c. Risk seeker.
    d. Risk positive.

12. What is the shape of the utility of wealth function for a risk-averse individual?
    a. Linear.
    b. Curving upward at a decreasing rate.
    c. Curving upward at an increasing rate.
    d. None of the above is correct.

13. Which of the following is correct about the marginal utility of wealth for a risk-neutral individual?
    a. It is rising as wealth increases.
    b. It is falling as wealth increases.
    c. It remains constant as wealth increases.

    d. It is rising until a certain level of wealth is reached, and then starts falling.

14. Today stock *XYZ* is trading at $55 a share and a year ago it was trading at $45 a share. Find an annual realized return (as a percentage price change) and log return. (Round to the third decimal.)
    a. 18.182 percent, 16.705 percent.
    b. 18.182 percent, 16.092 percent.
    c. 22.222 percent, 20.067 percent.
    d. 22.222 percent, 21.504 percent.

    To answer questions 15 through 20, use the following scenario. You were following the price of *XYZ* stock for a month. The closing prices for weeks 1, 2, 3, and 4 were $45, $46, $45.5, and $47, respectively. (Round your answers to the third decimal.)

15. Find weekly return for weeks 2, 3, and 4.
    a. 2.222 percent; −1.087 percent; 3.297 percent.
    b. 2.222 percent; −1.087 percent; 2.445 percent.
    c. 2.148 percent; −1.112 percent; 1.587 percent.
    d. 2.148 percent; −1.065 percent; 1.327 percent.

16. Find weekly log return for weeks 2, 3, and 4.
    a. 1.985 percent; −1.622 percent; 2.762 percent.
    b. 1.985 percent; −1.434 percent; 2.961 percent.
    c. 2.198 percent; −1.093 percent; 3.244 percent.
    d. 2.198 percent; −1.566 percent; 2.112 percent.

17. Find average weekly return and annualized return based on the three weeks of data.
    a. 1.323 percent; −56.522 percent.
    b. 1.477 percent; −76.821 percent.
    c. 1.477 percent; −53.224 percent.
    d. 1.323 percent; −45.322 percent.

18. Find the average weekly log return and annualized log return based on the three weeks of data.
    a. 0.941 percent; −52.147 percent.
    b. 0.941 percent; −48.922 percent.
    c. 1.450 percent; −75.374 percent.
    d. 1.450 percent; −54.998 percent.

19. Find the average weekly variance of returns based on the three weeks of data.
    a. 0.000348.
    b. 0.000524.
    c. 0.001019.
    d. 1.001223.

20. Assuming that one-week returns are uncorrelated, find the *annualized* variance of returns based on the three weeks of data.

    a. 0.020524.
    b. 0.011019.
    c. 0.018097.
    d. 0.055460.

21. Which of the following is correct about the risk-free rate?
    a. It is a return that the market pays you for postponing your consumption.
    b. It is an additional return that you get for investing in the risky asset.
    c. It is calculated as a difference between the risk premium and a total return.
    d. None of the above is correct.

22. The expected return on a market portfolio is 8 percent and the risk-free rate is 2.5. What is the risk premium offered in the marketplace?
    a. 10.5 percent.
    b. 5.5 percent.
    c. 2.5 percent.
    d. 8 percent.

23. You invested 30 percent of your wealth in the market portfolio and the rest in the risk-free asset. The expected return and standard deviation of the market portfolio are 8 percent and 5 percent. The risk-free rate is 3 percent. Find the expected return and the standard deviation of your combined portfolio.
    a. 5.9 percent; 0.9 percent.
    b. 2.4 percent; 1.5 percent.
    c. 4.5 percent; 1.5 percent.
    d. None of the above is correct.

24. Compared to the points lying on the capital market line, all points that lie above it are _____ and all points that lie below it are _____.
    a. Inferior; unattainable.
    b. Unattainable; inferior.
    c. Unattainable; unattainable.
    d. None of the above is correct.

25. Suppose that the capital market line goes through the risk-free rate r_f and the point M which corresponds to the market portfolio. If your indifference curve is tangent to the capital market line in the area that is above point M, you will be:
    a. Lending some amount at the risk-free rate and some other amount at the rate offered by the market portfolio.
    b. Borrowing some amount at the risk-free rate and some other amount at the rate offered by the market portfolio.
    c. Borrowing some amount at the rate offered by the market portfolio and lending some amount at the risk-free rate.

  d. Borrowing some amount at the risk-free rate and investing some amount at the rate offered by the market portfolio.

26. Suppose that the capital market line goes through the risk-free rate of 3 percent and the point M, which corresponds to the market portfolio with an expected return of 13 percent and a standard deviation of 5 percent. Which of the following is true about the portfolio with a expected return of 10 percent and a standard deviation of 6 percent?
  a. It lies above the capital market line and therefore is unattainable.
  b. It lies below the capital market line and therefore is inferior to the points on the line.
  c. It lies above the capital market line and therefore is inferior to the points on the line.
  d. It lies below the capital market line and therefore is unattainable.

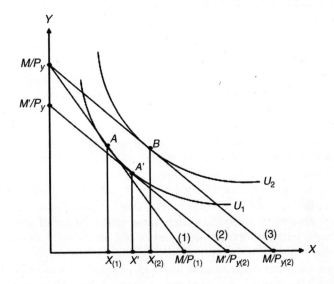

   Refer to the graph and the following scenario to answer questions **27 and 28.** The graph depicts the optimal consumption of goods X and Y and illustrates the income and substitution effects associated with the unit price of good X changing from its initial value of $P_{X(1)} = 3$ to the new lower value of $P_{X(2)} = 2$ and the optimal consumption basket shifting from point A to point B. Assume that consumer's income M is 120, unit price of good Y is $P_Y = 5$, and points A, A' and B correspond to 12, 10, and 12 units of good Y, respectively. Answer the following questions.

27. How many units of good X are consumed at point A and point B?
    a. 10; 25.
    b. 20; 30.
    c. 20; 40.
    d. None of the above.
28. Assuming that $X' = 24$, what is the income and substitution effect as measured in units of good X?
    a. 6; 4.
    b. 14; 1.
    c. 4; 16.
    d. None of the above.

APPLICATIONS AND ISSUES

1. Our equities market model, which we have used to illustrate utility to the consumer in current versus future consumption and risk appetites, makes specific assumption so that we can present the microeconomic principles. In considering the application of the principles set forth in our equity markets consumer choice model—budget constraints, substitution and the indifference curves, risks and uncertainty, and the risk-return trade-off—we have placed emphasis on measurements of these parameters. An attentive student might ask whether these somewhat elegant formulations are particular to the equities markets or whether they apply in all micro markets.

   In Chapter 1 we touched on the architectural design of the equities markets and the role of the market participants. While equities markets are a wonderful model, as they have high volumes of transactions and many participants, the question of the attentive student remains: do other markets respond in similar fashion? In our equities market model our investors have sought to build portfolios so as to optimize their needs for present and future consumption as well as to balance their individual risk appetites. We can apply these microeconomic principles in many similar markets to understand the price and quantities available for an economy.

   Rather than considering investors approaching the equities markets seeking to optimize their consumption and risk appetites, think of an architect approaching the markets for building materials with which to construct a building for his or her client. The client has specified certain requirements of location, size of "usable" space, and other occupancy characteristics. Yet it is the architect who designs the structure of the building. The building materials have constantly changing prices, quantities, and availability characteristics. The architect must consider all of the above in providing the client with a cost within their budget constraints. Engineering data will illustrate the principles of "load" bearance, resistance to wear and corrosion, sound dampening, and other characteristics of the different materials to be considered for the building.

The architect and the architect's client may have measured the distance of potential building sites to their present facilities, customers, and transportation, and may have taken the mean and standard deviation of those distances to appreciate the relative optimum in selecting a building site. Similar measurements will have been made of the risks of using different building shapes and materials. While for purposes of using this model, we may have assumed a "frictionless" operating environment, we all can recognize that the building will have costs of operation in utilities, insurance, taxes, and management, which for illustration purposes we will not consider. Finally, different construction methodologies, reinforced concrete, steel skeleton, low-rise prefabrication, and so forth will have different effects on the time needed to construct the building. Therefore, there will be a risk of materials availability and a trade-off among the alternative construction methods.

Finally, the architect will have to approach the micro markets for building materials. She or he will have to check whether the government's highway program reduced the availability of concrete. Also, as with Boston's "Big Dig," are the concrete suppliers reliable? Thereby she or he will reduce uncertainty, but not eliminate risk. The choice of whether to clad the building in masonry or glass may be determined by the prospects for the price of electricity for heating and cooling. Wood flooring may be pleasing, but its cost of installation and maintenance will be higher than that of asphalt linoleum. The micro markets for all of these building materials and their substitution one for another can be evaluated cumulatively as an indifference curve.

The point to be emphasized is that our discussion of the microeconomic principles using our equities market model should be seen by an attentive student as our exemplitive presentation of these principles. The challenge for the astute microeconomist in command of market microstructure principles is to see the principles in operation in markets for all scarce resources and consumption goods and services.

2. Should government entities assist the equities and other markets in assuring truly competitive and virtually frictionless market operations?

Philanthropy

Consider the following:

1. In microeconomic theory, utility maximization is the goal of a representative consumer (household).
2. Utility is a function of the goods and services that the decision maker consumes.
3. Some people give money, time, goods, and services to others and to charitable organizations.

Are these three statements mutually consistent?

If your goal is to maximize your utility, if your utility is a function of your personal consumption, and recognizing that the amount you can consume is greater when your income is greater, why give your income away? Is the act of giving irrational economic behavior? Or, are we being too restrictive by implying that your utility is a function only of your own personal consumption? Perhaps. Let's bring charity into the picture.

The more formal term for charity is *philanthropy* (from the Greek, meaning "love of man"). But not all giving is philanthropic. Giving might also be motivated by a desire for self-promotion, a kind of personal advertising expenditure, a statement that "I am a good person, I am an important person." Nevertheless, some people are concerned about the welfare of others and they give because they care. Can our utility-theoretic formulation handle this?

Incorporating philanthropic behavior into the utility-theoretic framework could not be simpler. We do so by introducing the concept of an *interrelated utility function*. That is, your utility is a function not only of your own consumption, but also of the consumption of others because you care about the welfare of others. This can be formalized.

In Chapter 2 we analyzed consumer choice by keeping it simple, by working in a two-product (or product characteristic) world (X and Y, current consumption and future consumption, risk and return). Let's continue to do this. Simply divide all consumption into two categories: the amount that the philanthropist consumes and the amount that a recipient of the charitable act consumes. Call the philanthropist A and the recipient B. Then A's utility function can be written as

$$U^A = U^A\left(C^A, C^B\right)$$

where C^A and C^B are A's and B's consumption, respectively.

We invite you to do the following with this background information.

1. Construct an indifference curve mapping for household A that has A's income and consumption on the horizontal axis, and B's income and consumption on the vertical axis.
2. Add a budget constraint to your diagram. To do so, let Y^A and Y^B be A's and B's income, respectively, and use Y^A and Y^B to locate the height of the constraint. The slope of the budget constraint is the negative of the price to A of a dollar's worth of personal consumption relative to the price to A of increasing B's consumption by one dollar. If A giving away a dollar results in B receiving a dollar, the slope of the budget constraint is -1.
3. Let D^{AB} be A's *donation* to B. Use your diagram to identify A's equilibrium amount of personal consumption and the optimal gift, D^{AB}, that A should give to B.
4. Note the similarity between the diagram that you have just produced and the present consumption, future consumption diagram in Exhibit 2.5.
5. Use your diagram to verify that D^{AB} is a positive function of Y^A/Y^B.
6. Present an indifference curve mapping which shows that if Y^A/Y^B is small enough A would be better off receiving a gift from B even though for $Y^A \geq Y^B$, A's attitude toward B, on the margin, is philanthropic.
7. Let MT be A's marginal tax rate and assume that A's gift to B is tax deductible (as some giving is). How is A's budget constraint affected? What effect does tax deductability have on giving rates? What effect does an increase in tax rates have on giving rates?

ADDITIONAL READINGS

Friedman, Benjamin M. *The Moral Consequences of Economic Growth*. New York: Knopf, 2005.
    The ethical arguments in favor of market-driven economic growth and its beneficent consequences to society.
Fusfeld, Daniel. *The Age of the Economist*. New York: Addison Wesley, 2002.
    A concise history of market-driven economics.
Sowell, Thomas. *On Classic Economics*. New Haven, CT: Yale University Press, 2006.
    A summary commentary of the major arguments supporting reliance on markets' pricing.

ANSWERS TO REVIEW QUESTIONS

1. c
2. d
3. c
4. d
5. d
6. b
7. a
8. d
9. b
10. b
11. c
12. b
13. c
14. c
15. a
16. c
17. b
18. c
19. a
20. c
21. a
22. b
23. c
24. b
25. d
26. b
27. b
28. a

Demand Meets Supply

LEARNING OBJECTIVES

- **Understand the formal derivation of the demand curve for a product or asset.** Chapter 3 extends the comparative static analyses presented in Chapter 2 to obtain continuous, downward-sloping demand curves for a consumer. The individual demand curves are aggregated to obtain a downward-sloping demand curve for the market. Graphical representations of both individual and market demand curves show the relationship between price and quantity, with price (the independent variable) on the vertical axis and quantity (the dependent variable) on the horizontal axis. You will see that, as the price of a product or asset increases (or decreases), demand decreases (or increases). In other words, the demand curve is downward sloping. You will also see that, by interfacing a downward-sloping market demand curve with an upward-sloping market supply curve, we can obtain an equilibrium solution for the two variables (price and quantity).

- **Appreciate the importance of elasticity, our measure of sensitivity.** We study an individual's demand for a resource (e.g., X) as being a function of several independent variables: the price of X, the price of a related good (Y), and income (M). Be certain to understand that elasticity, our sensitivity measure, is a measure of relative *percentage* changes. For instance, the elasticity of demand for X with respect to any one of the variables (e.g., P_X), is the percentage change in the quantity of X demanded divided by the percentage change in P_X. You will see elasticity classified and used in various ways in the chapter, and you will come to appreciate that the price elasticity of demand for a product (X) reflects how close two products, X and Y, are as substitutes for one another.

- **Be able to make the transition from individual demand curves to a market demand curve.** You will see how we aggregate individual demand curves to obtain the demand curve for the market. The transition from an individual demand curve to a market demand curve is quite straightforward for most resources, but you will appreciate that it is a bit more complex for a financial asset such as equity shares.

■ **Take a first look at the supply curve of a resource.** You will see a graphical representation of the relationship between price and quantity, with price (the independent variable) on the vertical axis, and quantity (the dependent variable) on the horizontal axis. As the price of an economic resource increases, the supply will increase, and the graphical relationship you will be looking at will be upward sloping. At this stage of the analysis, we only ask that you accept the upward-sloping supply curve as being intuitively reasonable. The supply curve is derived more formally in Chapter 5, and you will also find out that under some conditions it actually may not be upward sloping.

■ **Understand how equilibrium values for price and quantity are discovered for a product or asset.** You will see that, by interfacing the market demand curve for a resource with the market supply curve for that resource, we can identify the point where the forces of demand and supply are in balance. That point is where the two curves intersect. Economists call the value of the price coordinate at the point of intersection an *equilibrium price*. You should appreciate that if, in a perfectly competitive market, a price is above its equilibrium value, supply will increase, demand will be curtailed, and the unbalanced pressures of demand and supply will push price down to its equilibrium value. Or, if a price is below its equilibrium value, the unbalanced pressures of demand and supply will push price up to its equilibrium value.

■ **Recognize that an intervention in price and output determination can have undesirable consequences.** You should appreciate that if a market price is kept from reaching its equilibrium value (by, for instance, the imposition of a price ceiling or a price floor), the quantity demanded on the market will not equal the quantity supplied, and the larger of the two quantities will have to be rationed. You will also see how the imposition of a sales tax or subsidy will perturb the free market price and quantity equilibrium.

■ **Be able to apply the demand-supply structure to the market for a risky financial asset.** As we turn to the market for a financial asset, certain terms and details of the marketplace change, but the basic analytic approach remains the same. With a financial asset, we consider the trade-off between two attributes of the asset (risk and return) rather than the trade-off between two different resources (e.g., X and Y). With a financial asset, the price of risk is return, and the decision maker does not pay the price, but receives it. We trust that you will find this financial market an intriguing one to analyze from a microeconomic perspective.

CHAPTER SUMMARY

Our number-one objective in this chapter has been to understand how price and quantity are set in a marketplace that comprises a large number of buyers and sellers (large enough, that is, so that no one participant has any significant presence in the market and no one, therefore, can affect a market-determined price). In addressing this issue, we have continued to assume that the marketplace is a frictionless environment and, in so doing, we have built on the consumer choice model presented in the previous chapter. The following steps that we have taken are key:

1. We extended the comparative static results of Chapter 2 to obtain the decision maker's demand curve for a good or service, and for a financial asset. In so doing, we specified the relevant price for the economic resource under consideration, and the set of other variables that are constant along a demand curve. Throughout, we have taken tastes (the decision maker's utility function) as constant and, for simplicity, have assumed a two-good universe. For a generic product, the demand curve shows how the quantity of the product demanded (X) depends on its price (P_X), the price of the other generic product (P_Y), and the decision maker's money income (M). A change in P_X (all else constant) causes a movement along the demand curve, while a change in either of the other two demand determining variables causes the demand curve for X to shift.

2. Elasticity was introduced as the measure of X's responsiveness to each of the independent variables (with the other two variables being held constant). We identified three elasticities: own price elasticity (the responsiveness of X to its own price), cross price elasticity (the responsiveness of X to the price of the other product), and income elasticity (the responsiveness of X to the income variable). Complementarity and substitutability between X and Y were discussed with reference to X's own price elasticity, and to X's cross price elasticity with respect to Y. Clearly, relative prices are of greater importance to the decision maker, the better the substitutability between the two goods.

3. The demand curves of individuals were aggregated to obtain the demand curve for a market. Aggregation is a simple process: Sum up the quantities demanded by each of the individual participants at each of the different values of price.

4. The demand analysis was next applied in a more defined context. Building on the risk and return formulation presented in Chapter 2, we obtained the demand curve to hold shares of a risky asset in a two-asset environment (the risky asset and a risk-free asset). The risky asset was viewed as a market portfolio that comprises the full set of individual

stocks. Unlike the generic good, X, which is flow-dimensioned, the demand to hold shares of the risky market portfolio is stock-dimensioned. We worked in the context of a single period (e.g., one-year) model. The risk-free rate of interest [r_f] and the expected future price of the market portfolio [$E(P_T)$] constant, the demand to hold shares of the risky asset is a negative function of the current share price (P) of the risky asset. This is because, as P decreases, the risk premium $\left[\frac{E(P_T)}{P} - 1 - r_f\right]$ rises, and so a risk-averse investor will seek to hold a larger number of shares.

5. Returning to the generic product, X, we matched the market demand curve for X with a market supply curve of X to obtain the equilibrium values of price and quantity. The important properties of a supply curve were identified and the intersection of a downward-sloping demand curve with an upward-sloping supply curve was shown to establish a stable equilibrium price and quantity of X.

6. We then saw how regulatory intervention in the market for X can distort the free market price and quantity equilibrium. In particular, we considered the effects that can attend a government-imposed price ceiling, or a price floor, or a sales tax or subsidy.

7. Returning to the market for shares of the risky asset, we applied demand-supply analysis to obtain equilibrium in the marketplace where shares of the risky asset are traded. We clarified that in this setting there is only one demand curve: the demand to hold shares of the risky asset. From this curve, for an individual, we obtained two other curves: a downward-sloping curve to buy shares at lower prices, and an upward-sloping curve to sell shares at higher prices. It was the individual buy and sell curves that we summed across investors to get aggregate market buy and sell curves, and we matched these aggregates to establish the number of shares that would trade, and the price that they would trade at in the market.

8. We concluded the chapter with the thought that, in the frictionless environment, it is not portfolios or individual shares that are priced, it is risk that is priced. But one does not buy risk. Rather, the market pays a participant for accepting it. In the perfect, frictionless environment, perfect substitutes exist for every individual stock, and the market's demand curve to hold shares of each stock in the market portfolio is infinitely elastic at a price that depends on the stock's covariance with the market. This is because only systematic (as distinct from diversifiable) risk is priced (diversifiable risk can be reduced to nil by sufficient portfolio diversification), and a stock's covariance with the market measures the stock's systematic risk, which is the stock's contribution to the riskiness of the market portfolio (our risky asset).

GLOSSARY

complements Products that are consumed in combination with each other. If X and Y are complements, the cross elasticity of demand for X with respect to the price of Y is negative. Tennis rackets and tennis balls are complements. With perfect complements, X and Y are consumed in fixed proportions regardless of their relative prices.

covariance with the market A measure of how the rate of return for an asset varies with the rate of return on the market portfolio.

cross price elasticity The percentage in the quantity demanded or supplied of a good or service divided by the percentage change in another product's price, all else constant.

diversifiable risk The portion of the total returns variance for an asset that can be eliminated by portfolio diversification.

income elasticity of demand The percentage change in quantity for a good or service divided by the percentage change in a consumer's income, all else constant.

income expansion path For a two good model (e.g., X and Y), the locus of optimality points in X, Y space achieved by a consumer for different values of the consumer's income, the prices of X and of Y given (i.e., constant). For a consumer, the locus of all tangency points between a family of indifference curves and a set of parallel budget constraints that represent different levels of income.

nondiversifiable risk The portion of the total returns variance for an asset that is correlated with the returns on the market portfolio and thus cannot be eliminated by portfolio diversification.

normative economics An economic formulation that is purposed to prescribe how an individual participant (household or firm) ought to respond.

own price elasticity The percentage change in the quantity demanded or supplied for a product divided by the percentage change in that product's own price, all else constant.

positive economics An economic formulation that is purposed to predict (as opposed to prescribe) how a representative market participant (or all participants in aggregate) will respond to a change in an economic variable.

price ceiling An externally imposed, maximum price. A ceiling is effective if placed below a free market equilibrium price.

price floor An externally imposed, minimum price. A floor is effective if placed above a free market equilibrium price.

rectangular hyperbola A functional relationship between two variables, X and Y, where their product, XY, is a constant (e.g., $Y = aX^{-1}$). Average fixed costs (Y) as a function of output (X) is an example of a rectangular hyperbola.

representative consumer or supplier An individual participant in the market who, in playing the role of an average, represents all participants. Predicting the response of a representative participant to the change in an economic variable is equivalent to predicting how all participants in aggregate will behave.

socially desirable results Economic outcomes that optimize the allocation of scarce resources.

substitutes Products that are substituted for one another as relative prices change. If X and Y are substitutes, the cross elasticity of demand for X with respect to the price of Y is positive. Tea and coffee, for instance, are substitutes. With perfect substitutes, only X or only Y is generally consumed, depending on which is less expensive.

CURRENT EVENTS DISCUSSIONS

1. Do Substitutes and Complements Determine a Market's Architecture?

As we consider the actions of buyers and sellers in the stock markets, it is most important to recall that all markets respond in similar fashion to the needs and tastes of buyers/consumers and the opportunities and costs of sellers/producers. Wholly different markets for the factors of production may have different architectures, locations, and rules and regulations, but they all serve the process of price-setting and resource allocation. Understanding the microstructure of different markets can be generalized as we have done with our model of the stock market. Here are two news reports that discuss the price performance of two key commodities, copper and nickel. In some industrial applications copper and nickel are substitutes, and in some others they are complements. The point is that they respond to supply and demand. Demand is price elastic, and elastic to substitution, while supply is subject to cross price elasticity.

China Copper Need Set to Rise

China has become the world's largest copper user, accounting for roughly a quarter of global consumption, so its appetite for the red metal has a significant impact on prices. China's copper imports had tapered off, but some metal analysts believe China will return to a more normal industrial production after many plants were shut down to avoid air pollution ahead of the [Olympic] Games.

Others look for China's demand to eventually rise, because industry will have to resume stocking after running down inventories. While prices have dropped, which could boost demand, economic growth there appears to have slowed, which might curb buying.

The country's imports of refined copper during the first half of 2008 fell 23% on the year to 687,013 metric tons, according to Chinese data. Observers cited several factors that account for the slowing of Chinese copper-import demand, starting with an inventory drawdown when global prices were high. Much of that slowdown of imports into China is due to the fact they have been living off of their own domestic stockpiles of copper. It appears those stockpiles are starting to decline significantly. Typically, they have stepped in and started buying when we've seen a big sell-off.

Three-month copper on the London Metal Exchange fell from highs of $8,880 a metric ton in April and $8,940 in early July to an August low of $7,120. Similarly, nearby Comex copper on the New York Mercantile Exchange dropped from a lifetime exchange high of $4.27 a pound to a low of $3.2350. On Friday, September copper settled at $3.4725, down 7.35 cents.

The recent narrowing of the spread of higher London Metal Exchange prices over Shanghai Futures Exchange prices also increases the likelihood of more imports into China, observers said.

China's copper use was dented when slowing global economies meant less demand for the country's exports, said Brian Hicks, comanager of U.S. Global Investors' Global Resources Fund. Instead, much of China's copper consumption is for development of electricity-generating capacity, they said. "There is a power shortage taking place," Mr. Hicks said, "and a lot of that copper is going to go into the electric grid."

—*The Economist* (August 8, 2008)

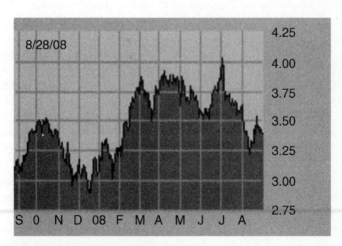

Spot Copper (dollars per pound)
Source: © BigCharts.

High Costs Dig into Mine Profits

As Nickel Falls, BHP Faces Long Road for Australian Project

Weaker commodity prices and higher costs are starting to take a toll on the global mining industry as the billions of dollars being spent on new projects could take years to recoup.

For years, BHP Billiton Ltd. assured shareholders that one of its biggest new mines, an Australian nickel project called Ravensthorpe, would be a big moneymaker. Now, with production underway, the Melbourne, Australia-based mining company says Ravensthorpe isn't profitable though it will do well eventually. But with nickel prices down 60% from mid-2007 highs and mining costs spiraling higher, some analysts wonder if Ravensthorpe will ever make much money at all. At least three other mining companies have curbed output or delayed expansions because of softer prices and higher costs. Analysts believe more will follow.

The turnaround highlights an important change in the world's mining industry. A few years ago, demand was rising so quickly, and supply was so tight, that almost any new project seemed attractive.

Since then, costs have surged and demand has started to wane. As a result, analysts say, some of the newer and higher-cost mines coming online are likely to struggle to deliver returns—even if demand for commodities continues to boom. Costs for miners vary widely depending on location of the mine, quality of the ore and local tax regimes, making it difficult for investors to pick out which projects could face risks in the new environment.

BHP, which has some of the biggest iron-ore reserves in the world, recently reported annual earnings of $15.4 billion, up nearly 15%. Demand for resources by China and other emerging markets still is expected to soar in the years ahead.

Some analysts view the recent mine closures as bullish for commodity prices in the long run, because the moves suggest companies are imposing more financial discipline than in past booms. As miners curb output, it could help prop up prices.

Still, the economics of mining have shifted drastically in recent years. The cost of energy to run mining trucks and other equipment has skyrocketed, while steel and other building materials also are more expensive. Nickel producers are also being squeezed by rising costs of sulfuric acid, a key component for processing some types of nickel ore. Sulfur prices have rocketed from an average of just more than $100 a ton last year to more than $800.

Another issue for miners is that as commodity prices rose, customers began finding ways to cut back on consumption, such as using raw-material substitutes. Builders are using plastic pipe in place of copper, and stainless-steel producers are turning to "nickel pig iron" made from low-grade mineral ores.

As a result, "we now believe nickel is below the marginal cost of production" for many mines, says John Reade, a metals analyst at UBS in London.

While it is only a tiny part of BHP's overall business, Ravensthorpe is the kind of project that could get squeezed. BHP managers announced the project, which is centered on a mine in southwestern Australia, in 2004. A company official at the time touted the project's "low mining costs" and said it offered "just about the best risk-reward profile" of any similar nickel project in the world. Its estimated cost: $1.4 billion.

Some investors questioned the project because of its complex refining process. In late 2006, BHP increased Ravensthorpe's budget to $2.2 billion as material and labor costs ballooned, but noted that the project was "well-positioned to deliver positive results." Soon after, the price of nickel hit all-time highs of more than $20 a pound.

Ravensthorpe began initial production in late 2007, with plans to ramp up to full capacity by 2010. But by early 2008, nickel fell to about $12 a pound—and was heading lower. On Friday in London, the three-month nickel contract closed at $9.50 a pound.

The project isn't currently making money, a representative said. But the company and some industry analysts believe it will become profitable as costs are paid down.

BHP often doesn't break out detailed information on costs at its mines. But Chief Financial Officer Alex Vanselow said last week that the project would ultimately need nickel prices within a range of $5 and $8 a pound—probably at the bottom of the range—to break even.

—Wall Street Journal (August 25, 2008), p. A1

Questions

1. For a class discussion using the above two articles:
   a. Describe the following aspects of the demand for copper.
      - Who are the major consumers of copper?
      - Where are the major supplies of copper located?
      - What metals or other materials are substitutes for copper?
      - What are the major processes and their costs in converting copper ore to usable copper?
   b. As the chairperson of the Chinese Ministry of Metals, you have been requested to report to the Central Committee of the Chinese Peoples

Republic on what policies you would recommend be adopted to constrain the demand for copper. The Committee meets next Monday.

c. The major uses for nickel include the use as an alloy in the production of stainless steel, and the use in the minting of coins. It is said that the marginal rate of substitution from monetary purposes to industrial purposes can be illustrated graphically. For class discussion, prepare a graph which clearly identifies the price point at current prices of the marginal rate of substitution for both copper and nickel.

2. In the allocation of scarce resources we have suggested that market prices send "signals" to both consumers and producers. The trends of prices for basic commodities of foods, fuels, metals, and labor and capital signal growing demands, external shocks, scarcities, and excesses of supply. The article below discusses the forces that bear upon raw materials prices for an extended period. Clearly market participants seek to formulate their own views as to future prices and act accordingly. In turn, governments periodically intervene in markets to restrain "price volatility" for such basic commodities. Please read this with the idea in mind that you may be asked your views as to what the markets "signals" and their consequences are.

Endurance Test

Some Reasons Not to Expect a Collapse in Raw-Materials Prices

During the six months to the end of June commodities posted their best performance in 35 years, rising by 29%. In July they had their worst month in 28 years, falling by 10%. The slide continues: an index compiled by Reuters, a news agency, shows that prices are almost a fifth below the pinnacle reached in early July. The Economist's index, which excludes oil, has fallen by over 12%. Breathless headlines have hailed the bursting of a bubble.

But most analysts are more reticent. They cite various reasons for the recent drop in prices, chief among them the darkening economic outlook in rich countries. In recent weeks it has become clear that Europe and Japan are faring even worse than America, and so are likely to consume less oil, steel, cocoa, and the like. But that does not necessarily presage a collapse in commodity prices, they argue, thanks to enduringly strong demand from emerging markets such as China.

Oil consumption, for example, has been falling in rich countries for over two years. Goldman Sachs expects them to use 500,000 fewer barrels a day (b/d) this year than last. But it reckons that

decline will be more than offset by an increase of 1.3m b/d in emerging markets. It predicts China's demand for oil will grow by 5%.

A similar story could be told of many commodities. Marius Kloppers, the boss of BHP Billiton, a huge mining firm presenting its results this week, argued that emerging markets were much more important to the firm's fortunes than rich ones were. Developing countries, he said, consume four to five times more raw materials per unit of output than rich ones do. He predicted that China's use of steel, already greater than any other country's, will double by 2015. China's continuing and rapid industrialisation, he argued, would outweigh any temporary slowdown in exports owing to the weakening world economy—although demand for metals that are used in consumer goods, such as aluminum and nickel, may suffer somewhat.

As Mr. Kloppers pointed out, emerging markets, and China in particular, now account for the lion's share of growth in global demand for raw materials, and a good chunk of overall consumption (see chart). China's appetite for such goods is growing more slowly than it did in the early part of the decade—when oil consumption galloped ahead by more than 10% a year. And China's economy has also slowed slightly—although it is still growing at a rate of about 10%. The IMF expects developing countries to grow by almost 7% this year. That should be enough to keep demand for most commodities expanding briskly.

In terms of supply, however, the picture is more mixed. Farmers, encouraged by high prices, have been planting more grain. Heavy rains in America's farming heartland earlier in the year did less damage to crops than expected. The International Grains Council, an industry group, now expects a record wheat crop this year, 9% bigger than last year's. China and India, meanwhile, have produced record amounts of soybeans, while Thailand and Vietnam have harvested bumper crops of rice. Although stocks of most farm commodities remain alarmingly low, and demand continues to grow, the increasing evidence of a strong supply response has helped to push prices down.

The world's output of industrial metals is also expanding, and prices have been dropping for over a year. But progress has been fitful. At many mines, the quality of the ore is falling as the richest seams are exhausted. Mr. Kloppers spoke of BHP's woeful shortage of tires for its huge trucks, big mechanical shovels, bearings and all manner of other equipment. Such bottlenecks have been hampering the opening of new mines and the expansion of existing ones. *Kona Haque of Macquarie Bank points out that copper mines have produced 1m tons or so less than planned in each of the past three years (over 5% of global output), and are likely to do so again this year.*

High commodity prices have created something of a vicious circle by adding to the expense and difficulty of expanding output. This week, Xstrata, another big mining firm, suspended operations at a nickel mine in the Dominican Republic while converting its power supply to run on coal, rather than—more expensive—oil. Power shortages have disrupted mining and smelting in several countries. The Chinese government has started to discourage the expansion of energy-intensive industries, including aluminum and steelmaking, in an effort to ease the burden on its grid. All this is hampering the production of metals around the world, and so slowing the fall in prices.

Nonetheless, the output of most metals is still growing much faster than that of oil—which is barely expanding at all. The oil industry, too, is suffering from shortages of equipment and engineers. Even worse, all of the countries best equipped to pump more of the stuff are members of the Organization of the Petroleum Exporting Countries (OPEC).

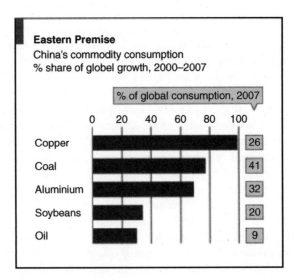

Source: Barclays Capital.

Saudi Arabia, the cartel's biggest producer, has increased its output in recent months, even as the rich economies, still the largest consumers of oil, slowed. That helped to push the price down from $147 a barrel to less than $115. Despite a rise in American inventories, global stocks do not appear to have grown much, suggesting that buoyant developing economies absorbed most of the increase in supply. Meanwhile, more hawkish members of OPEC, such as Venezuela, are calling for a cut in output to stop oil prices falling further. When OPEC last cut production, early in 2007, prices doubled in just over a year.

Other factors also influence commodity prices. Some see commodities in general, and gold in particular, as a hedge against inflation, and so may sell if their fears about rising prices abate. Other investors may sell to cover losses in other markets, or to rebalance their portfolios in light of falling share and bond prices, or to avoid the wrath of America's politicians, who have vowed to crack down on "speculation". Commodities also tend to move in the opposite direction to the dollar, which has risen of late. All that notwithstanding, argues Francisco Blanch, of Merrill Lynch, as long as economic growth holds up in the developing world, the price of commodities should too.

—**The Economist**, August 21, 2008

Questions

1. For a class discussion, select several major raw materials and chart their price movements for a recent period of at least 20 years. Evaluate the forces that led to significant price changes. Indicate your appraisal of the current prices for the selected raw materials. Finally, as an informed market participant, set forth your views of the "mid-term" (six months to three years) price prospects for these raw materials.

2. Governments regularly "stockpile" critical "strategic" materials such as petroleum, metals, chemicals, and flu vaccines. These are held against future emergencies, such as when natural disasters or war actions limit the supplies of these materials. As the government's Director of Emergency Planning, what acquisition programs for these strategic materials would you recommend? In answering, place particular focus on the consequences to market prices for these materials. Be prepared to present your program recommendations to the Secretary of Defense by early next week.

REVIEW QUESTIONS

1. The sensitivity of quantity of X demanded to a price of some other good is called
   a. Own price elasticity.
   b. Cross price elasticity.
   c. Substitute price elasticity.
   d. Complementary price elasticity.
2. In a consumer choice model, if goods X and Y are perfect substitutes, the X, Y indifference curves are
   a. Downward sloping and linear.
   b. L-shaped.
   c. Downward sloping with a moderate curvature.
   d. Upward sloping and linear.
3. Goods X and Y are complements if the cross price elasticity is
   a. Positive; that is, the consumption of good X decreases if the price of good Y increases.
   b. Positive; that is, the consumption of good X increases if the price of good Y increases.
   c. Negative; that is, the consumption of good X decreases if the price of good Y increases.
   d. Negative; that is, the consumption of good X increases if the price of good Y increases.
4. If good A and good B are complements, an increase in the price of good A would
   a. Have no effect on the quantity demanded of B.
   b. Lead to an increase in the quantity demanded of B.
   c. Lead to a decrease in the quantity demanded of B.
   d. Lead to good B's demand curve shifting to the right.
5. Which of the following would not shift an individual's demand curve for good A?
   a. A change in price of good A.
   b. A change in price of good B (good B is a substitute for good A).
   c. A change in the consumer's income.
   d. A change in the amount of advertising for good A.
6. Which of the following is consistent with the stability of an equilibrium price?
   a. If the price moves up from its equilibrium value, the resulting excess supply will create an upward pressure.
   b. If the price moves up from its equilibrium value, the resulting excess supply will create a downward pressure.

c. If the price moves down from its equilibrium value, the resulting excess demand will create a downward pressure.

d. If the price moves down from its equilibrium value, the resulting excess supply will create an upward pressure.

7. Which of the following relationships reflects the impact of a price floor?
   a. $X^D < X^* < X^S$.
   b. $X^D > X^* > X^S$.
   c. $X^D > X^S > X^*$.
   d. $X^* < X^D < X^S$.

8. Which of the following best describes the changes in the price of X and the quantity of X exchanged in the market after an imposition of a sales tax (assuming a downward-sloping demand curve and an upward-sloping supply curve)?
   a. The quantity of X will increase, the price paid by buyers will decrease, and the price received by sellers will decrease.
   b. The quantity of X will remain unchanged, the price paid by buyers will increase, and the price received by sellers will decrease.
   c. The quantity of X will decrease, the price paid by buyers will decrease, and the price received by sellers will decrease.
   d. The quantity of X will decrease, the price paid by buyers will increase, and the price received by sellers will decrease.

9. Which of the following statements is normative as distinct from positive?
   a. To boost competition, government should interfere in the workings of the free market as little as possible.
   b. If money supply is increased, interest rates should go down.
   c. Government subsidy of an industry should result in a larger quantity of the industry's good being produced and consumed.
   d. None of the above statements is normative.

10. Which of the following is true about the market demand and the market supply curves to hold shares of a risky asset?
    a. The demand curve is downward sloping and the supply curve is upward sloping.
    b. The demand curve is vertical and the supply curve is upward sloping.
    c. The supply curve is vertical and the demand curve is upward sloping.
    d. The supply curve is vertical and the demand curve is downward sloping.

11. Market demand curve for wheat can be obtained by adding the quantities demanded by all individual participants at each level of price, which is a
    a. Horizontal summation of individual flow-dimensioned demand curves.

    b. Vertical summation of individual flow-dimensioned demand curves.

    c. Horizontal summation of individual stock-dimensioned buy curves.

    d. Vertical summation of individual stock-dimensioned buy curves.

12. Systematic risk is

    a. A component of the stock's total risk that arises due to the factors that affect all (or most) stocks in the market.

    b. A component of the stock's total risk that arises due to the factors that are unique to a given stock.

    c. Also referred to as diversifiable risk.

    d. Both **b** and **c** are correct.

13. An individual investor's demand curve to hold shares of a risky asset

    a. Is downward sloping and reflects investor's risk-aversion; that is, a higher risk premium is necessary to induce an investor to hold more shares.

    b. Is downward sloping and its intercept with the vertical axis is at a value that implies a zero-risk premium.

    c. Is vertical because the number of shares of stock outstanding is fixed.

    d. Both **a** and **b**.

14. In a CAPM framework

    a. The marketplace is frictionless.

    b. Investor expectations are homogeneous.

    c. An individual investor can borrow/lend unlimited amounts at a constant rate of interest, r_f.

    d. All of the above are correct.

15. In a competitive market, the market demand is $X^d = 60 - 6P$ and the market supply is $X^s = 4P$. A price ceiling of \$3 will result in a

    a. Surplus of 30 units.

    b. Shortage of 30 units.

    c. Surplus of 12 units.

    d. Shortage of 12 units.

APPLICATIONS AND ISSUES

1. Our discussion of the operations of markets for products has emphasized the equities markets and the demand elasticities of common stocks as they are priced in the equities markets. Some of our discussions have reflected on the particularities of the equities markets, such as stock splits, portfolio diversification, and rates of return. As we consider other products, materials, labor markets, and the markets for the factors of production, we need to ask whether the particularities of the equities markets can be generally applied to other markets. In general

the answer is *yes*. Yet we also should recall that the architectures of different markets are often different. As we have emphasized with the equities markets, the primary risks are price declines driven by the economic performance of the company, of the sector, or of the entire equities market.

In markets for labor, the risks taken by the consumer (the firm hiring the worker) include the honesty of the worker, the worker's ability to master the methods of the hiring firm, the currency or obsolescence of the worker's skills, and the health of the worker. Therefore, the labor markets adapt its architecture to contain these risks to an acceptable level. Such adaptations include government-sponsored programs for labor such as "equal employment opportunity," Social Security, disability income, Medicaid, and retraining assistance. In addition, the labor market provides for consumer protection (for the firm) in state and local statutes, assuring "hiring at will" to permit the termination of the risk of a failed asset (worker). Sellers in the labor market may choose to "fix" prices by forming unions and bargaining with firms collectively.

The dissimilarities between the equities and the labor markets are exemplified by certain structural differences between the two markets. In the first instance, labor markets are highly fragmented with high levels of product differentiation, for example, entry level workers as opposed to senior executives. Further, in a world of "globalization" consumers may wish to expand the market to permit the "outplacement" of work, or "outsourcing" of product (workers). Finally, consumers seek to diversify their portfolios of products (workers) so as to assure continuity and reduce the risk of product failure.

Just as technology has changed and accelerated obsolescence has added complexity to the equities markets, the same has also occurred in the labor markets. The rapid evolution of Internet-based employment services has virtually eliminated prior patterns of operation in the labor markets. Such services include inventories of available job opportunities, search engines to find job opportunities that match sets of interests/skills, and research browsers for "background" information on both consumers (hiring firms) and producers (workers.) Collectively these technological changes have transformed the labor markets into sensitive, risk-averse, and rapid pricing mechanisms for all levels of labor.

As a discussion exercise, it would be productive to consider the similarities and contrasts between the equities and the labor markets. Such an exercise should concentrate on the issues of "elasticities," "substitutes," "complements," and "socially desirable results."

2. In recent years, investors have had increasingly more of the alternative forms of investment. In 1929, at the time of the great stock market "crash," less than 15 percent of American households owned common equities. It is estimated that today the number of households owning stock (through mutual funds, ESOPs, Incentive Stock Options, etc.) is in excess of 60 percent. Similarly, nonfarm home ownership has expanded from less than 30 percent to almost 70 percent of American households since 1929. The two great areas of investment for American households have been equities and real estate (including land.) Households' real estate may be highly leveraged (funded with mortgages, second mortgages, and home equity loans).

Government sponsorship of household real estate investment takes many forms: tax incentives, mortgage agencies, guarantees, and little regulation. Conversely, government sponsorship of household equities investments is discouraged in a variety of ways, including SEC disclosure requirements, tax penalties for withdrawals from investment funds (IRAs, 401ks, Keogh Plans, etc.), margin requirements limiting leverage, and the double taxation of dividend income.

As a discussion exercise, it would be enlightening to consider these two household investment markets, equities and real estate, giving specific differentiation to the architecture of both markets.

ADDITIONAL READINGS

Fischer, David H. *The Great Wave: Price Revolutions and the Rhythm of History*. New York: Oxford University Press, 1996.

    A historical discussion of the microeconomic drivers of the major "surges" in commodity pricing in Western civilization.

Friedman, Milton and Rose. *Free to Choose*. New York: Harcourt Brace, 1990.

    A classic political polemic in favor of market determining micro- and macroeconomics.

Greenfield, Liah. *The Spirit of Capitalism*. Cambridge, MA: Harvard University Press, 2001.

    A polemic advocacy of the advantages of market capitalism over its alternatives.

ANSWERS TO REVIEW QUESTIONS

1. b
2. a
3. c
4. c
5. a
6. b
7. a
8. d
9. a
10. d
11. a
12. a
13. d
14. d
15. b

CHAPTER 4

Microeconomic Analysis Goes to Market

LEARNING OBJECTIVES

- **Understand the contrast between short-run and long-run demand and supply.** Because adjustments take time to make, demand and supply responses are both more price elastic in the long run than in the short run. Therefore, a supply shift or demand shift will have a larger proportionate effect on price relative to quantity in the short run, and a larger proportionate effect on quantity relative to price in the long run.
- **Appreciate the importance of adjustment costs.** Adjusting some consumption patterns and asset holdings in a nonfrictionless environment is not a trivial matter. An array of transaction costs (commissions, fees, information costs, implicit execution costs, legal expenses, and so on) affect participants' decisions and reduce the benefits they get from trading.
- **Gain insight into the operations of brokers and dealers.** These market participants are the sellers of trading services. When they trade with the public as principals they are called dealers or market makers, and when they handle public orders as agents they are called brokers. You should understand the special services that they provide, the unique costs that they incur, and how they are paid for their services.
- **Understand how transaction prices are determined in a securities market, how quotes are established, and the importance of the bid-ask spread.** In this chapter, you will come in contact with different market structures. You will deal with both dealer quotes and the quotes set by public limit orders. You will understand that the market spread is the difference between the lowest posted offer (also referred to as "the ask") and the highest posted bid. You will see that the spread for a company's stock will widen or tighten depending on factors such as the

stock's price, its volatility, and the frequency with which information about the company changes.

- **Appreciate the importance of liquidity for the efficient functioning of a market.** Liquidity is a slippery term to define, but we generally have a pretty good sense of what it means—the ability to buy or to sell at a reasonable price, in a reasonably short amount of time, in reasonably large quantities. Liquidity is similar in spirit to elasticity. If a market is liquid, a large buy order, for instance, can be executed with only a minimal price impact; if supply, for instance, is price elastic, a small increase in price will attract a sizable increase in supply. Many markets, ranging from houses to the equity shares of medium- and small-capitalization stocks, are not very liquid and, consequently, trading in them is relatively difficult.

- **Recognize differences in the architectural structures of different markets, and appreciate that market structure matters.** From supermarkets and art auctions to securities exchanges and the housing market, real-world markets are structured in any number of ways. While basic economic formulations (such as our demand/supply analysis, for instance) may be applicable to a broad range of markets, they are devoid of specific institutional content and so do not take account of a market's unique architecture. In this chapter, we do. Specifically, we consider four different generic structures that are germane to financial markets. You should gain insight into the unique workings of a quote-driven dealer market, a continuous-order-driven agency market, a periodic-order-driven call auction, and a negotiated block market.

- **Appreciate the difficulty of getting, and importance of achieving, sufficiently accurate price discovery and sufficiently complete quantity discovery.** It is one thing to interface a downward-sloping demand curve with an upward-sloping supply curve and say that their intersection identifies the equilibrium price and quantity for the market; it is another matter for these two values to be found in a marketplace. Price discovery is the process by which a market clearing, equilibrium value is found, and it is not a simple task when participants employ trading strategies and are not all in the market all of the time. Quantity discovery is the process by which the conterparties to a trade find each other, and it is not a simple task when the counterparties do not reveal their presence or the total amount that they are seeking to buy or to sell. You will see the complexities of price and quantity discovery as they pertain to trading in an equity market.

- **Identify the gains from trading.** A trade that two parties freely undertake must be beneficial to both of them. This chapter shows how the gains from a trade might be quantified. For a buyer, we call the gain *consumer surplus*; for a seller, the term is *producer surplus*. Consumer surplus is the maximum amount the consumer would be willing to pay for the entire amount purchased, less the (smaller) amount actually paid. Producer surplus is the total amount actually received, less the minimum (smaller) amount the seller would be willing to receive for the entire amount sold. These gains from trading are used to assess the cost of any intervention that keeps price and quantity from attaining equilibrium values. You will see that the concept of a trading surplus is also useful for formulating trading strategies and for assessing the effect of market design on trading strategies and outcomes.

■ **Be aware of various strategic decisions that trading can involve.** Various questions can be raised when going to a market to trade. Should I buy now or wait for a better price? Should I pay now or buy on credit? Should I place a limit order or a market order? And so forth. The limit order versus market order decision is particularly germane to an equity market, and the chapter considers it. The chapter also raises the question of whether to submit an order to a call auction, or to a continuous market, or to both. Comprehending the nature of these strategic decisions is important for understanding the dynamic operations of a micro market, and the role that is played by a market's architecture.

CHAPTER SUMMARY

Our goal in this chapter has been to build a bridge between the theoretical properties of the frictionless environment that we have considered in Chapters 2 and 3, and the realities of actual markets that we have all experienced. In doing this, we have devoted major attention to the secondary markets for already-issued equity shares. Here are the six highlights:

1. Friction in the economic environment is clearly reflected in one distinction that microeconomists have long made—the difference between short-run and long-run equilibrium solutions. Because of adjustment costs, short-run quantity responses to changes in economic variables are partial, and thus are less elastic than long-run quantity responses. In considering this, we discussed adjustment costs in general and trading costs in specific. In order to hone in on trading costs, we identified eight key terms: quotations, bids, offers, limit orders, market orders, spreads, short selling, and arbitrage trading.

2. Liquidity, a term that is difficult to define but quite easy to recognize, is of critical importance to a market. Illiquidity and trading costs are in certain respects two sides of the same coin. Much economic analysis

abstracts from illiquidity issues by assuming a frictionless environment, and that is where we started our discussion of microeconomics. But as we moved away from the perfectly liquid market, we introduced price discovery and quantity discovery as two economic objectives of major importance, and we underscored the important role that market structure plays in achieving acceptably accurate price discovery and acceptably complete quantity discovery.

3. With the importance of market structure established, we turned to alternatives for market structure itself and, once again, focused on the equity markets. We saw how prices are established and trades are made in quote-driven (dealer) markets, in continuous-order-driven (limit order book) agency markets, in periodic-order-driven call auctions, and in negotiated (block) markets.

4. With an overview of alternative market structures established, our attention returned to an individual trader's participation in the market. The first item of business was to quantify a participant's gains from trading. Our measure of this, for a buyer, is *consumer surplus*, a term that we defined with the use of two demand curves (the ordinary demand curve that we have thus far been working with, and a reservation demand curve.) For a seller, the analogous term is *producer surplus*. When referring to the gains of both buyers and sellers, we simply say "surplus."

For a buyer, a reservation price is the maximum that he or she would be willing to pay for a specific quantity of the good in question when the alternative is to get nothing at all. Consumer surplus, our monetary measure of the gains to trade for a buyer, is the difference between this maximum amount that he or she would pay (the reservation price) and the amount that he or she actually has to pay, times quantity. In making a trading decision, the order placer's objective is to maximize the expected value of the surplus (this is consistent with the maximization of his or her expected utility).

5. With the trader's objective established, we next considered his or her strategic order placement. The strategic decision has two parts: (1) the number of shares that you wish to trade has to be fixed, and (2) the price of your order has to be determined. We simplified the analysis by assuming that the number of shares in the order has already been determined, and then focused only on price. Of particular importance is our understanding of how micro markets and their participants operate. With this in mind, we contrasted two alternative market structures, (1) the continuous limit order book market and (2) the periodic call auction. We showed that the optimal order pricing decision of our representative participant differed between the two.

6. We concluded the chapter with "the big picture." Two statements merit reiteration:

- "In the nonfrictionless world, not all mutually beneficial trades are realized, market clearing prices can deviate from equilibrium values, market participants use trading strategies when they come to a market to trade, and the very strategies that they employ can further affect market outcomes." Quite clearly, models of frictionless markets require modification and further elaboration when applied to markets where trading is costly.

- "Transaction costs are endemic to the micro markets. Short-run demand and supply curves in all markets are less elastic than their long-run counterparts because adjustments are not easy to make. Multi-year contracts, other lengthy time commitments, and protracted building and construction periods all impact the workings of the micro markets." Consequently, issues such as price and quantity discovery that we have considered with respect to the equity markets may also be germane to other markets, in which the long run is measured not in hours or days, but in years.

GLOSSARY

arbitrage trading   The coordinated trading of two or more assets stocks that are mispriced vis-à-vis each other, for instance, the purchase of a relatively low-priced stock and the simultaneous short sale of a relatively high-priced stock. The arbitrageur profits as the prices of the two stocks converge (as the spread between them shrinks).

arbitrageur ("arb")   An investor who specializes in arbitrage trading.

ask quotation   The price at which someone is willing to sell shares.

bid quotation   The market posted price at which someone is willing to buy shares.

bid-ask spread   The gap between the lowest quoted offer that has been posted on the market and the highest quoted bid that has been posted.

brokers   Sell-side participants who handle orders for their customers as agents. Brokers typically receive commission payments for their services.

buy-side customers   Investors who require the services of sell-side intermediaries to get their trades done. Institutional investors such as mutual funds, pension funds, and hedge funds are buy-side customers.

call auction   An order-driven market that provides periodic rather than continuous trading. All submitted orders are cleared at the same point in time at the same price in one big, generally multilateral trade. Electronic calls are commonly being used to open and close trading sessions.

clearing price   The price set in call auction trading at the time when the market is called and the price is set. The clearing price is typically the value that would maximize the number of shares that trade. Equivalently, the clearing price is the value that best balances the cumulated buy and sell orders that have been submitted to the call. Buy orders that are equal to or higher than the clearing price execute, as do sell orders that are equal to or lower than the clearing price.

consumer surplus   The (larger) total amount that a purchaser (consumer) would be willing to pay for X units of good (the purchaser's reservation price times X) less the (smaller) total amount that has to be paid (the market price for X times X), because the market price for X is less than the purchase reservation price for X.

continuous trading   An order-driven or quote-driven market where a trade can be made at any point in continuous time that the price a buyer is willing to pay (or that a seller is willing to receive) crosses a price that someone else is willing to receive (or is willing to pay).

dark liquidity pools   Trading facilities where the buy and sell orders of participants are not disclosed. Opaque markets.

dealers   Sell-side participants who trade with their customers and, in so doing, take principal positions. Dealers typically receive their compensation from the bid-ask spread.

elastic price demand   A percentage change in price induces a greater percentage change in the quantity demanded.

execution costs   The implicit costs of trading; for instance, bid-ask spreads and market-impact costs.

explicit costs   The direct costs of trading; for instance, commissions and taxes.

indicated clearing price   the call auction price that is displayed to the public while orders are being entered into the auction during its book-building phase. The indicated clearing price is the value that the clearing price would be if the book were to be frozen and the market called at that moment; it is the value that would maximize the number of shares that would execute.

inelastic price demand   A percentage change in price induces a less than proportionate percentage change in the quantity demanded.

limit order   A priced order to buy or to sell a specific number of shares of a stock. For a buy order, the price limit is a maximum. For a sell order, the price limit is a minimum.

market bid-ask spread   The best (lowest) market ask minus the best (highest) market bid.

market makers   Dealers with an affirmative obligation to continuously make two-sided markets (i.e., to continuously post bid and offer quotes).

market order   an unpriced order to buy or to sell a specific number of shares of a stock at whatever the market price might be.

order-driven market   A market where public participants trade with each other without the intervention of a dealer (market maker). Limit orders posted by some public participants establish the prices at which other public participants can trade by market order.

periodic trading   Call market trading. *See* call auction.

price discovery   In any micro market, price discovery is the process of finding an equilibrium value for a good, service, or productive resource that is being traded. Price discovery is a complex, imperfect process when participants do not simultaneously reveal their complete demand and supply functions. In an equity market, price discovery is the dynamic process of finding a value that best reflects the broad market's desire to hold shares of a stock. In equity markets, price discovery occurs most prominently after the receipt of news and following market openings as prices adjust to new economic conditions and to changes in the investors' desires to hold shares.

quantity discovery The process of buyers' orders and sellers' orders meeting in the market and being turned into trades. It becomes a complex and incomplete process when buyers and sellers do not reveal their full trading intensions because they are afraid that doing so will cause adverse price effects. With quantity discovery incomplete, a latent demand to buy and to sell shares exists.

quotation A price at which someone is willing to buy or to sell shares, and the number of shares that the quote is good for. A quote can be either "firm" or "indicative."

quote-driven market A market where public participants do not trade directly with each other, but with dealers (market makers) who in posting their quotes establish the prices at which trades can be made.

reservation price The maximum price a customer would be willing to pay for a unit of a given quantity when the alternative is to obtain nothing at all. It is also the minimum that a seller would be willing to receive for a given quantity when the alternative is to sell nothing at all.

scaled order An order that is broken into two or more smaller pieces that are entered at two or more different prices. The submission of a downward sloping buy curve (or a subset of points along the buy curve) is a scaled order.

sell-side intermediaries Brokers and dealer who sell trading services to their buy-side customers.

short selling Selling borrowed stock on the expectation that a future decline in stock price will permit a subsequent (and profitable) purchase at a lower price.

strategic trading decisions The order placement decisions made by traders seeking to optimize their gains from trading.

two-sided quotes An agent such as a securities dealer simultaneously posts both a bid quote at which he or she will buy shares, and an ask quote at which he or she will sell shares.

upstairs market An off-exchange market (typically the "upstairs" offices of a bank or brokerage house) where negotiated trades can be effected.

CURRENT EVENTS DISCUSSIONS

Since its establishment in 1791, the New York Stock Exchange has evolved into one of the world's premier markets for U.S. equities. Founded for the purpose of trading U.S. government debt issues (stock) and later expanded to trade railroad securities, the NYSE's market architecture adapted to new securities and to new forms of trading. Shares of industrial corporations were rarely traded until the innovations in corporate public ownership by

J.P. Morgan at the end of the nineteenth century took place. The great stock market crash of 1929 brought substantial government oversight in the form of the Securities and Exchange Commission (SEC), and more vigorous self-regulation by the exchange. Below are two recent articles that illustrate the continued evolution of the equities markets.

1. Do Stock Exchanges Evolve and Face Competition as Do Other Markets?

Big Board, Nasdaq Face Competition from Upstart Firm

BATS Trading Inc. received approval from the Securities and Exchange Commission to operate a stock exchange that will compete more directly with NYSE Euronext's New York Stock Exchange and Nasdaq OMX Group Inc.'s Nasdaq Stock Market.

Closely held BATS, of Kansas City, Mo., says the BATS Exchange will open in about two months. The company already trades about 10% of the share activity on NYSE and Nasdaq-listed stocks, combined, illustrating the ability of upstart stock markets to take business away from established exchanges that have gone public and focused more on profits.

Launched in January 2006, BATS's electronic trading network has grown quickly by offering heavy discounts on trading fees and promises of faster execution of buy and sell orders. Its owners include affiliates of large banks and Wall Street brokers, including Citigroup Inc., Credit Suisse Group, Deutsche Bank AG, Lehman Brothers Holdings Inc. and Morgan Stanley. It also counts more than 340 firms as subscribers.

BATS, an acronym for Better Alternative Trading System, filed for exchange status in November 2007 after working on the application since early last year.

Operating as an exchange will enable BATS to send out price quotes more quickly and directly to customers. As an electronic communication network, or ECN, it currently disseminates quotes via the National Stock Exchange and the ISE Stock Exchange, a method that some say led to small delays.

"Our timeliness will improve dramatically" as an exchange, said Joe Ratterman, chief executive of BATS. "Our market share is starting to rival other exchanges, and it makes sense to be on the same playing field as our competitors." ECNs traditionally were "not mentioned in the same sentences as exchanges . . . we were like second-class citizens," Mr. Ratterman added.

BATS executives expect becoming an exchange will help the firm increase market share by three to five percentage points by the end of this year. Its longer-term goal is to reach 25% market share, making it much more of a threat to the established exchanges. In July, BATS traded an average of 969 million shares per day, which compares with the 2.9 billion U.S. shares that Nasdaq traded daily that month and 3.7 billion on the NYSE's systems. Those figures don't count the significant portion of trading activity that brokers conduct off exchanges.

An NYSE spokesman said "we welcome the competition," while a Nasdaq spokeswoman declined to comment.

BATS was founded by David Cummings, a computer programmer who was successful at developing trading strategies. BATS first began trading Nasdaq-listed stocks and later expanded to NYSE stocks.

"Anyone who can come up with 10% market share in two years is obviously a threat" to the larger exchanges, notes Michael Henry, a senior executive in the capital-markets practice at Accenture, the consulting firm. He adds that smaller trading networks, many of which are backed by banks, are claiming to be more nimble than large players at seizing market opportunities.

When it becomes an exchange, BATS may endure more regulatory requirements that slow down certain projects, however. It is adding about a dozen employees to increase its regulatory presence in order to become an exchange.

—Wall Street Journal (August 19, 2008), p. C3

Questions

1. As the capital markets for equities and other commodities respond to technological innovation and new securities products, new market places emerge. The worldwide Internet and fiber-optic networks have reduced the cost of communications and permitted an elimination of market location differences. For a class discussion, consider the possibility of creating a new marketplace for Credit Default Swaps. You might want to consider the following aspects of such a marketplace.

   ■ Who would be the major participants in such a new market?
   ■ What would be the pricing mechanism for such a market?
   ■ Which government agency would regulate this new market?
   ■ What would be the "lot" size of transactions?
   ■ Where would the optimal location for this new market be?

2. The proportion of the trading in "listed" equities that occurs on the New York Stock Exchange has dropped significantly in the last several years. As an expert in Market Microstructure you have been retained by the Board of Governors of the NYSE to examine this situation, and make recommendations for "correcting" the drop in its proportion. The Board will be meeting on Monday to hear your recommendations.

2. As Financial Markets Become More International, Will Stock Markets, like Other Markets, Become Global?

In addition to new securities exchanges being formed domestically, newly wealthy foreign locales also seek to establish securities markets. The following article describes such new markets in the Persian Gulf. In addition, newly industrializing nations such as India and China have expanded their well-developed securities exchanges.

Come Buy

Saudi Arabia opens its stock market, at last, to foreign investors. They are likely to take full advantage.

The gradual process of opening the Saudi stockmarket to foreign investors has taken a significant step forward with the announcement that non-residents will be entitled to trade in local stocks through Saudi intermediaries. The news prompted an immediate rally in the market—which has lost ground so far this year—in apparent anticipation of a surge in foreign interest. That optimism is well-founded, as there is plenty of value to be found on the Saudi bourse, which is by far the largest in the Middle East by market capitalisation, and most of the big names in global equity investment have a presence in Riyadh.

Share-Swap

The announcement from the Capital Market Authority (CMA) on August 20th stated that "authorised persons" (in other words local entities licensed by the CMA) may enter into swap agreements with non-resident foreign investors, both individual and corporate, to transfer the economic benefits of shares listed in the Saudi Stock Exchange (Tadawul). Legal ownership of the shares will reside with the Saudi intermediary.

According to a note issued by EFG-Hermes, a Cairo-based investment bank with a long-standing presence in Saudi Arabia, the

regulations covering the swaps are in place, but the CMA is review-
ing the structures and procedures offered by the Saudi intermedia-
ries before giving the go-ahead for the first actual deals. EFG-
Hermes indicated that swap agreements must be fully financed and
covered at the time of purchase, and are valid for a maximum four
years. Voting rights are retained by the Saudi parties, but they are
not permitted to exercise these rights. No limits have yet been set
on the proportion of free-float shares that a foreign investor may
own in a company or sector.

The swap arrangement is part of a process of opening up the
Saudi market that started with the approval of a number of off-
shore mutual funds in the late 1990s. In 2006, after the market
crashed in the second quarter, the CMA allowed foreign residents
to invest, and last year the market was opened up to citizens of the
Gulf Co-operation Council, and the CMA started issuing licences
to investment banks to set up brokerage, asset management and ad-
visory affiliates. The latest opening came at a relatively subdued
moment. The Tadawul all-share index (TASI) had fallen by more
than 20% since the start of the year, largely because of sell-offs to
enable investors to participate in a succession of initial public offer-
ings (IPOs)—the most recent was a US$2.5bn offering in shares in
Maaden, a mining company—and trading activity usually slows
down in Ramadan, the Muslim fasting month, which starts on Sep-
tember 1st. These appear to be favourable conditions for introduc-
ing a new system that is likely, eventually, to lead to a big increase
in trading volumes.

Varied Palette

A succession of IPOs over the past five years has resulted in the
number of stocks listed on the Tadawul almost doubling. There are
now 126 listed firms, with a total market capitalisation of
SR1.74bn (US$463bn) as of August 25th. Just over one-third of
the total issued shares are free-floating. Heavy industrial firms,
such as Saud Basic Industries (Sabic), account for almost 40% of
total market capitalisation, followed by banking, telecoms and real
estate. Tadawul classifies the listed firms in 15 sectors. The price/
earnings (P/E) of the market as a whole is currently 19.14, accord-
ing to Tadawul, based on 2007 income. EFG-Hermes reckons that
the forward P/E ratios are a rather more enticing 14.1 based on
projected 2008 earnings and 13.0 based on forecast 2009 earnings.
—The Economist Intelligence Unit ViewsWire (August 27, 2008)

Questions

1. A recent study by the New York University and Columbia University schools of business stated that the New York financial markets were losing a significant portion of the world's financial transactions and securities trading to other financial centers, including London, Frankfurt, Singapore, and Tokyo. Newly established trading venues such as that described above were further reducing New York's preeminence as the center of the world's capital markets. For a class discussion, consider the factors that have led to this trend, including your recommendation concerning the following:
   - The harsh American regulatory arena, which makes for a slowing of transactions.
   - The cost of doing business in New York.
   - The obsolete trading structure of the major New York exchange.
   - The rules of "full disclosure" which preclude business "privacy."

2. After completing your presentation to the Board of the New York Stock Exchange, your secretary tells you that the Emir of Oman is on the phone seeking your recommendations for his new exchange. You have also just received a ticket for a first-class seat on Emirate's Airlines new Airbus A380 flying to Dubai, where you are to advise the Emir. You have only 12 hours of flight time in which to prepare your recommendations for the optimal performance of the Emir's new Capital Markets Exchange.

REVIEW QUESTIONS

1. Which of the following is TRUE about the short-run and long-run supply and demand curves for a good X?
   a. Short-run curves are more elastic than long-run curves for both supply and demand.
   b. Long-run curves are more elastic than short-run curves for both supply and demand.
   c. Short-run curves are more elastic than long-run curves for demand, but not for supply.
   d. Long-run curves are more elastic than short-run curves for supply, but not for demand.

2. Which of the following is FALSE about the costs of trading?
   a. Explicit costs and execution costs are the two broad categories of the trading costs.
   b. Commissions and taxes are examples of explicit costs

    c. Execution costs, as opposed to explicit costs, are implicit.

    d. Execution costs are referred to as opportunity costs.

3. A market order

    a. Is a prepositioned order.

    b. Can execute against a dealer quote or a posted limit order.

    c. Is an unpriced order.

    d. Is both **b** and **c**.

4. Short-selling refers to

    a. Reducing long positions.

    b. Selling borrowed shares.

    c. Selling at prices below market.

    d. None of the above.

5. Which of the following is FALSE about the negotiated (block) market?

    a. It is a market venue used primarily by big institutional investors who are looking to execute large orders.

    b. In such a market, negotiation can be direct person-to-person or can take place through an electronic interface.

    c. Participants in such a market set their own price for the stock without much consideration for the price discovered in the main market (i.e., an exchange).

    d. From a market structure point of view, the raison d'etre of such a market is quantity discovery as distinct from price discovery.

6. What is the relationship between an ordinary demand curve and an associated reservation demand curve?

    a. An ordinary demand curve is less steep than its associated reservation demand curve.

    b. An ordinary demand curve is steeper than its associated reservation demand curve.

    c. An ordinary demand curve and its associated reservation demand curve intersect at the point of unit elasticity on the ordinary demand curve.

    d. Both **b** and **c** are correct.

7. For a call auction that is not followed by continuous trading, the optimal price for you to place an order for a given quantity is

    a. A weighted average of expected prices at which others will submit their orders.

    b. Your reservation price.

    c. The price that you expect the call to clear at.

    d. None of the above.

8. Consumer surplus at quantity X can be measured as a

    a. Unit price that you actually pay, times X.

    b. Height of the reservation demand curve at quantity X, times X.

    c. Height of the reservation demand curve at quantity X, minus the unit price that you actually pay, times X.

    d. Height of the ordinary demand curve at quantity X, minus the unit price that you actually pay, times X.

9. The limit order book is used in a
   - **a.** Quote driver, dealer market.
   - **b.** Call auction.
   - **c.** Negotiated (block) market.
   - **d.** Both **a** and **b**.

10. In an order driven market, a market order to buy will typically execute against
    - **a.** The lowest prepositioned market order to sell.
    - **b.** The lowest prepositioned limit order to sell.
    - **c.** The lowest ask price posted by a dealer in this stock.
    - **d.** The last order to sell posted on the market, regardless of its price.

11. Which of the following is TRUE about market makers?
    - **a.** They act in trading on behalf of their clients.
    - **b.** They are called buy-side intermediaries because roughly 50 percent of the time they act as a buyer in a transaction.
    - **c.** They are called sell-side intermediaries because they sell intermediary services.
    - **d.** When they face an inventory imbalance, they post a one-sided quote, that is, only a bid quotation or only an ask quotation.

12. In a call auction, a clearing price
    - **a.** Is set by a market maker at the level that maximizes its commission revenue from the call.
    - **b.** Maximizes the total number of shares that trade at the call, given the set of submitted orders.
    - **c.** Is the price that enables everybody who submitted an order execute fully at the call-determined price.
    - **d.** Both **b** and **c** are correct.

13. A riskless arbitrage trading refers to
    - **a.** Profiting from coordinated buying and selling of the same asset when it can be bought (in one market) at a price that is lower than it can be sold at (in another market).
    - **b.** Shorting the overpriced stock.
    - **c.** Buying the underpriced stock.
    - **d.** Buying a stock in an opening call auction and selling it at a continuous market that follows.

14. Which of the following is correct about a bid-ask spread?
    - **a.** It is also referred to as the BBO (best bid and offer).

    b. It represents the cost of a round-trip incurred by a market order placer, i.e., buying at the ask and selling at the bid.

    c. Half of the bid-ask spread is taken to be a cost of executing with immediacy that is incurred by a market order placer when buying or selling.

    d. All of the above are correct.

15. Which of the following situations represents an active trader?

    a. An investor places a market order to buy shares.

    b. An investor places a limit order to sell shares.

    c. A market maker posts bid and ask quotes.

    d. None of the above.

APPLICATIONS AND ISSUES

Why Do Bid-Ask Spreads Exist in Securities Markets?

In the earlier part of this chapter we identify the bid-ask spread as a cost of trading. Later in the chapter we focus on the trading strategy an investor might employ when going to an equity market to buy or to sell shares. Can these two topics be tied together? Could it be that investor trading strategies explain the existence of bid-ask spreads in a securities market? This is the issue that we address with our thought question for this chapter.*

A single list price is commonly specified for many of the goods and services that we buy. But in some cases there are two prices: a higher offer price that is extended to buyers and a lower bid price that is extended to sellers. Spreads are typical of quote-driven, dealer markets (for instance, currency dealers, securities dealers, and used-car dealers) where there are public customers on both sides of the market, with some people looking to buy while others are looking to sell. In these markets, the existence of spreads is easy to understand. A dealer firm is an intermediary who stands between the natural sellers and the natural buyers and therefore it must set its purchase price lower than its selling price, because the difference is the source of its profits.

If there is no dealer intermediary, does the spread disappear? What if buyers and sellers can meet and trade without the services of a dealer? If we

---

*Material in this question draws from Kalman Cohen, Steven Maier, Robert Schwartz, and David Whitcomb, "Transaction Costs, Order Placement Strategy, and Existence of the Bid-Ask Spread," *Journal of Political Economy* (April 1981), 287–305.

turn to an order-driven market, will there still be a bid-ask spread? The answer is not obvious. Consider a limit order book such as the one shown in Exhibit 4.4. Let a very large number of participants arrive at the market, look at the book, and enter either a limit order or a market order. As more limit orders arrive, the book fills.

In Exhibit 4.4, there are no buy limits at 10.40, 10.20, and 9.90, and there are no sell limits at 10.90, and 11.30; if a fistful of new limit orders were to arrive, these "air pockets" in the book would fill in, and they would do so simply by chance. Another vacant price point is seen in the exhibit at 10.70. This one is within the spread. Will it disappear like the air pockets, or is its existence systematic? With a large enough number of participants entering limit orders, any price point between the bid and the offer would fill unless the absence of orders within the spread is systematic. That is what we have to figure out.

An analytical context is needed to answer this question. Assume a single stock that is traded in an order-driven equity market; an arbitrarily large number of participants; that each participant is looking to buy or to sell just one round lot of 100 shares (with an order size that is the same for all, we can ignore the possibility of partial executions); that price is a continuous variable (unlike the discrete prices shown in Exhibit 4.4); that participants each have a reservation price to buy or to sell shares; and that each participant has a single objective—maximize his or her expected gains from trading. With this by way of background, we ask you to address the following.

1. Consider an individual buyer with a reservation price of 12.00 who is coming to the market at a time when the best (lowest) offer on the market is 10.80. What is the buyer's gain from trade if he or she submits a market order to buy one round lot? (Remember, a round lot is 100 shares.)

2. What is the buyer's *expected* gains from trade if, instead of submitting a market order, he or she submits a limit order at 10.70 and the probability that the limit order at this price will execute is 0.95?

3. Given your answers to 1 and 2 above, which order should the buyer place, the market order or the limit order at 10.70?

4. How would you answer question 3 if the buyer were to place the limit order at 10.78? (Remember, for our analysis price is a continuous variable, so 10.78 is a possible price point.) Let the probability that the limit order at 10.78 will execute be 0.96.

5. Back away from the numbers for a moment. In general, how do the potential gains from trading by limit order change as the limit order gets placed ever closer to a counterpart market ask that could be hit with certainty by a market order? As the price of the limit order gets

infinitesimally close to the counterpart market ask, do you agree that, if the order executes, the gain from trading by the limit order becomes infinitesimally close to the certain gain from trading by market order? Of course, if the limit order does not execute, no gain from trading is realized at all.

6. But what about the probability that the limit order will execute? How does it change as the limit buy order is placed ever closer to the market ask at 10.80? Clearly, the probability that the buy order will execute is higher, the higher is its price. But the following is key: As long as the buy order is placed below the market ask, no matter how close to the ask it might be (even infinitesimally close), the probability that the order will execute remains discretely below one.

Some math is needed to prove the point we have just made, but the concept can be grasped intuitively. Suppose your limit order is placed infinitesimally below the offer and is sitting there when some bullish news comes out. The limit sell order(s) at 10.80 will most likely be withdrawn as quickly as possible, a higher ask will be posted, and your limit buy order will look more unattractive to the sellers. Does this make intuitive sense to you? Can you see that, no matter how close your buy limit is to the offer, because you have not actually *lifted* the offer with a market order, you are taking a risk, and you are facing a finite probability that your order will not execute? Can you appreciate that there is a qualitative difference between trading with certainty (submitting a market order), and without certainty (i.e., not submitting a market order that would consummate the deal)?

7. So, what is the story for a limit order that is placed just a hair below the counterpart sell order of 10.80 that is on the book? Quite clearly, the gain from the limit order is virtually identical to the gain from the market order, but the probability of the limit order executing does not get infinitesimally close to 1. So, here is the question: Will the buyer ever post a limit buy order infinitesimally close to an already-posted offer? Reciprocally, will a seller ever post a limit sell order infinitesimally close to an already-posted bid? What do you think?

8. Do you see why we have assumed that price is a continuous variable? Do you understand why the spread will never be infinitesimal when price variations can themselves be infinitesimal? Can you generalize the result and appreciate that, when price is not a continuous variable, empty price points can endure within the spread (such as the one at 10.70 in Exhibit 4.4) even when an arbitrarily large number of participants are placing limit orders on the book? So, there we have it. The empty price points within the spread are

systematic. Do you see that this result is attributable to the trading strategies of participants, to their appreciation of the value of trading with certainty?

9. Apply the thinking developed thus far to a bargaining situation. Suppose two people are haggling over the sale of a secondhand car that is priced in the $2,000 to $3,000 range. How close can their bid and offer get before the two negotiators will simply say, let's split the difference and consummate the trade? Would they keep bargaining when they are within $200 of each other? When they are within $100? Within $50, or less? Recognizing that they would both get surplus from the trade, do you agree that they will settle on a price long before the spread between them gets narrowed down to $1?

10. As you know, two quotes establish the spread: the lowest of all the ask quotes, and the highest of all the bid quotes. For the spread to endure, the best bid and the best offer must be far enough away from each other so that neither the buyer nor the seller is attracted to switch to a market order strategy, accept the counterpart quote, and trade. In other words, all posted limit orders must lie outside the "gravitational pull" of the counterpart quotes. Alternatively stated, no limit order will be posted within the "gravitational pull" of a counterpart quote. What exerts the gravitational pull? The attractiveness of trading with certainty. Can you understand why we have explained the existence of bid-ask spreads with the use of the term "gravitational pull"? Does this use of an astronomical term make sense to you? Can you accept that the configuration of counterpart quotes on a limit order book must, in equilibrium, maintain sufficient space between the buys and the sells, just as the configuration of satellites, planets, and stars must preserve sufficient space between these heavenly bodies or else they will collide?

11. Pull it all together and answer the question that we started with: Why do spreads exist in securities markets? And go further: Explain which of the following are expected to have larger spreads: a $100 stock or a $20 stock? A large-cap, frequently traded stock, or a low-cap, infrequently traded stock? A stock that experiences frequent information change, or one that does not?

12. Relax the assumption that all orders are for one round lot and consider the possibility of a large buy order and a large sell order being on the book at the same time. How would the size of the spread between the two large orders compare, on expectation, with the size of the spread between the smaller buy and sell orders?

Frictions in the Executives Markets

As in our prior chapters, we are now challenged with projecting the principle set forth in our discussion of the equities markets and their specific architecture to other markets for factors of production and consumer goods. The discovery of price and quantity are functions of all effective free markets. Yet we also understand that there are frictional costs, both explicit and implicit, in these functions. One sector of the labor markets is the market for executive talent, or as economists refer to it, management skill. The rigors of graduate business education and finance are some of the "listing" requirements for individuals seeking a "bid" in this market. Further, there are market imperfections or frictions that impede discovery, such as "glass ceilings" and experiential internship preferences. In particular, it is alleged that these frictions have operated to preclude a truly "free market" for executive talent.

For a class discussion, consider, compare, and contrast the characteristics, architecture, and participants in the executives market, including intermediaries of the equities market and the executive talent "call auction."

ADDITIONAL READINGS

Hunt, E. K. *Property and Prophets*: *The Evolution of Economic Institutions*. Armonk, NY: M.E. Sharpe, 2003.

> The evolution of markets, capitalism, its institutions, and the attendant critiques and defenses.

Jensen, Michael C. *A Theory of the Firm: Governance, Residual Claims and Organization*. Cambridge, MA: Harvard University Press, 2000.

> An examination of the market demand for enterprise management, its conflicted interest with owners, and methods to provide for the resolution of these conflicts.

Koehn, Nancy F. *Brand New: How Entrepreneurs Earned Consumer Trust*. Cambridge, MA: Harvard Business School Press, 1995.

> A set of cases illustrating innovative entrepreneurial activity responding to customer utility and preferences.

McMillan, John. *Reinventing the Bazaar: A Natural History of Markets*. New York: W.W. Norton, 2002.

> An accessible history of the American equity markets.

Schwartz, Robert A., and Reto Francioni. *Equity Markets in Action*. Hoboken, NJ: John Wiley & Sons, 2004.

> A comprehensive survey of the operations of the equity markets, their movements, and the nuances of trading.

ANSWERS TO REVIEW QUESTIONS

1. b
2. d
3. d
4. b
5. c
6. b
7. b
8. c
9. b
10. b
11. c
12. b
13. a
14. d
15. a

Supply and the Costs of Production

LEARNING OBJECTIVES

- **Appreciate the dominant importance of cost management.** Firms producing and distributing goods and services in competitive markets have little control over the prices established in their respective markets. All that they can control are their costs and the quantities of output that they produce. Accordingly, competitive firms concentrate on the efficiency with which they use their factors of production, for this is the road that leads them to maximum profits. You should understand from Chapter 5 in the Micro Markets text how this works in a simplified setting that enables us to derive fundamental principles concerning the supply of a good or service.

- **Understand a firm's production function and its related isoquant mapping.** To examine a competitive firm's output decision, we must first evaluate the relationship between the resources it employs (its factors of production) and the quantity of the product or service that the firm is producing. For this purpose, Chapter 5 introduces you to a firm's production function. A production function describes technology, much as a utility function describes tastes. From a firm's production function, we obtain a family of isoquants (where "iso" means "equal," and "isoquant" means an equal amount of output). A firm's isoquants play a role in production theory that is similar to the one played by indifference curves in consumption theory.

- **Appreciate the role that a firm's production function, isoquants, and factor costs play in obtaining the supply curve of a competitive firm.** By interfacing a firm's isoquant mapping with a set of iso-cost curves (which are equivalent to a household's budget constraint), we can determine how to efficiently combine factor inputs to achieve any given level of output. With this information in hand, we can proceed to the firm's cost curves and, from there, to the competitive firm's supply curve.

■ **Understand two conditions that must be satisfied for a firm to maximize its profits, (1) the least cost combination of factors of production condition and (2) the best profit output condition.** The least cost combination condition is satisfied when factor inputs are used in a combination that is given by a point of tangency between an isoquant curve and a isocost curve. When this condition is satisfied, total cost is minimized for any given level of output, and total output is maximized for any given level of expenditures. With this accomplished, we can proceed to a firm's cost curves (achieving a least cost combination of factors minimizes the height of a firm's cost curves). The best profit output condition is satisfied by operating at an output rate where marginal cost equals marginal revenue, and where price is greater than average variable cost.

■ **Comprehend the meaning of increasing, constant, and decreasing returns to scale.** The term "returns to scale" applies to (long-run) movements along a line called an *expansion path* that is given by the various points of tangency between a firm's isoquants and its isocost curves. If, as the firm moves along its expansion path, total output increases at a faster pace than total costs, the firm is operating under conditions of increasing returns to scale. If output and costs increase proportionately, the firm is operating under conditions of constant returns to scale. If costs are rising faster than output, then the firm is operating under conditions of decreasing return to scale. You should understand the reason why a competitive firm, in long-run equilibrium, will always operate under conditions of decreasing returns to scale.

■ **Be sensitive to the difference between fixed and variable costs.** Fixed versus variable costs are discussed in Chapter 1 of the textbook. In the short run, some costs are fixed (for instance, in relatively brief intervals of time contracts cannot be easily renegotiated and plant size cannot be easily changed), and some costs are variable (for instance, office supplies and materials can be readily attained and new workers hired). In the long run, all costs are variable. You should understand that only variable costs are relevant for decision making, but that profits, of course, reflect all costs (fixed as well as variable).

■ **Know the role that average costs and marginal costs play in determining a firm's best profit output decision.** Marginal analysis is also discussed in Chapter 1 of the textbook. Decisions are made on the margin. For any firm, the best profit output is the rate where marginal cost equals marginal revenue. For a competitive firm, the best profit output is where marginal cost equals marginal revenue *equals price* (having no power to affect price, marginal revenue for the competitive firms is price).

■ **Be able to graph the cost curves of a representative firm.** A firm's total cost curve is obtained from information given by its isoquants and isocost curve mappings. From these mappings we get the total cost curve. You should understand how the average and marginal cost curves are obtained from the total cost curve. For short-run analysis, you will see what the average fixed cost, output relationship looks like. For the short-run, long-run contrast, you should understand how the long-run average cost curve, as an envelope function, contains a family of short-run average cost curves, and how the long-run marginal cost curve and family of short-run marginal cost curves fit into all of this.

■ **Be able to make the transition from the cost curves of a competitive firm to that firm's supply curve and, from there, to the aggregate supply curve of a competitive industry.** You should understand that the firm's supply curve is its marginal cost curve above and to the right of the minimum point on its average cost curve. With one exception, the industry supply curve is simply the sum of the individual firm supply curves (just as an industry demand curve is the sum of the individual households' demand curves). The one exception is when economies or diseconomies of scale exist that are external to the individual firms but internal to the industry. You should further understand that a firm has a supply curve only when the demand curve that it faces is infinitely elastic (which means that marginal revenue equals price). To repeat: If price does not equal marginal revenue, the concept of a supply curve does not apply.

■ **Be able to apply the general principles covered in the earlier part of.** Chapter 5 in *Micro Markets* to the market for dealer services The learning objective here is to understand that a relatively abstract formulation can be applied in a relatively specific, real-world setting. Dealer firms, whether in a securities market, a commodities market, a used car market, one of the markets for building materials, or any other market, supply specific services, realize revenues in a specific way, and incur a unique set of costs. This part of Chapter 5 focuses specifically on equity securities dealers. It provides basic information about this market. It considers the nature of market maker services, revenues, and costs. It presents a dealer pricing model and brings you face-to-face with the challenge a dealer faces in dynamically controlling his/her inventory. You should understand why a dealer firm's average and marginal cost curves are expected to have the usual U-shape. For a competitive dealer market, you should understand why, with economies of scale that are external to the individual dealers but internal to the industry, the aggregate supply of dealer supported transactions not only is more elastic, but can actually be negatively inclined.

CHAPTER SUMMARY

In this chapter our focus has switched from the consumer side of the market to the producer side. We have considered production functions, cost curves, and supply curves (their counterparts from the consumer side are utility functions and demand curves). Having analyzed both the demand and the supply sides of the market, we are in a good position to investigate how competition plays out in a marketplace, the topic that we turn to in Chapter 6. Here are the 12 highlights of Chapter 5:

1. The starting point for supply analysis is a firm's production function—a technological description of how the factors of production that a firm uses can be combined in varying proportions to produce the good or service that it is supplying to the market. We first focused on our generic product, X. We simplified the discussion with no substantive loss of generality by dealing with just two productive factors, which we called "labor" and "capital."

2. Two sets of curves were defined: *isoquants* (each isoquant is the locus of all of the different labor and capital combinations that give the same output), and *isocost lines* (each isocost line is the locus of all of the different labor and capital combinations that require the same total expenditure). A firm makes its input and output decisions with regard to a family of isoquant and isocost lines. Wherever an isoquant is tangent to an isocost line, total production costs are minimized for that output and, reciprocally, total output is maximized for that cost. Accordingly, the tangency solution satisfies one requirement for profit maximization: the least cost combination of inputs condition.

3. The set of isoquant, isocost line tangency points defines an upward sloping line that is called the firm's expansion path (attributable to constant incremental increases in the inputs of labor and capital). If equal movements out along a linear expansion path result in increasing increments of output, the firm is operating under conditions of increasing returns to scale. If constant increments of output are realized for equal movements along the path, the firm is operating under conditions of constant returns to scale. If decreasing increments of

output are being realized, the firm is experiencing decreasing returns to scale.

4. Total cost is not a constraint for a firm in the way that a budget constraint is for a household. If a firm can use more inputs and produce a larger quantity profitably, it can operate at a higher level of expenditures. The equilibrium output level for a firm depends on the price that it can sell its product at, and on its production costs. The information needed to construct the firm's cost curves can be extracted from its isoquant, isocost line mapping.

5. We obtained the firm's long-run and short-run total cost curves. These were used to get the average and marginal cost curves. In doing so, we distinguished between fixed costs and variable costs.

6. With the firm's marginal and average cost curves in hand, we identified the second requirement for profit maximization: the firm's best profit output. Given that the least cost combination of inputs condition is satisfied, the firm's best profit output is the output level that equates marginal cost with marginal revenue, subject to average variable costs being less than average revenue (recall that for the competitive firm, average revenue is the product's price).

7. With the firm's marginal cost curve and best profit output identified, we established that the competitive firm's supply curve is its marginal cost curve above the minimum point of its average cost curve. The analysis was then extended in two ways. First, we showed how the supply curve for the industry is affected by economies of scale that are external to the individual firms but internal to the industry in aggregate. Second, we clarified that the marginal cost curve is the supply curve of the firm only for a perfectly competitive industry. You will appreciate as you read on that both of these extensions are important (the first was applied in the latter part of this chapter, and the second is germane to the chapter that follows).

8. Except for a concluding section, the remainder of the chapter considered how our cost and supply analysis applies to a dealer market. After providing some basic background information on this market, we identified dealer services (first and foremost, the provision of immediacy), dealer revenues (the classic source is the dealer's bid-ask spread), and dealer costs (the cost of carrying an unbalanced inventory and the cost of trading with a better informed investor). Each of these items (services, revenues, and costs) is unique to the dealer firms. More general economic analysis helps to understand them, but each requires special thought.

9. As you no doubt have noticed, microeconomic analysis typically involves the search for equilibria, and this is what we did with regard

to the dealer market. We first presented a simple pricing model for a monopoly dealer, and then considered a dynamic dealer pricing model.

10. Hand-in-hand with the dealer firm's dynamic pricing policy is its need to maintain reasonable bounds on its inventory fluctuations. With the firm's inventory policy depicted, we turned to a competitive dealer market and obtained a set of representative average and marginal cost curves for a competitive dealer firm. This derivation required some special thought, as the cost curves were not obtained from a dealer firm's production function. Nevertheless, the standard U-shaped average and marginal cost structures held for the competitive dealer firm. We made one adjustment, however. Rather than referring simply to output and costs, we operated in the space of the *expected* number of transactions and *expected* costs.

11. As noted above, we demonstrated earlier in the chapter how the supply curve for an industry is affected by economies of scale that are external to the individual firms in the industry, but are internal to the industry in aggregate. We applied this analysis to the industry's aggregate supply of dealer services. Economies are realized as the market for an individual stock grows—that is, as the total value of shares outstanding for an issue (referred to as the issue's *cap size*) increases: More information is available about larger-cap firms, their stocks' trading volume is greater, they trade more frequently, and the ratio of liquidity traders to information traders may be higher. All of this facilitates inventory management and cost control for the individual firms and, in so doing, shifts the firms' cost curves down, and increases the elasticity of the industry's aggregate supply of dealer services.

12. Having investigated how microeconomic analysis can be applied to the dealer market, we concluded the chapter with the following thought: "There is a method and a methodology for studying a micro market, but each market has its own unique characteristics. Thus thought has to be given to how the tools of microeconomic analysis can best be applied to any particular, real world market. This is all part of the fascination of the subject."

GLOSSARY

average fixed costs   A firm's total fixed costs divided by total output.

capitalization (cap) size   The total value of shares (the price per share times the number of shares) of the stock that is outstanding.

cost of ignorance　The cost to a dealer firm or limit order placer of trading with a better-informed participant.

dynamic dealer pricing　Adjustment made in a dealer's bid and ask quotes to control inventory imbalances.

expansion path　With the quantity of labor and the quantity of capital inputs on the axes, the expansion path is the line established by the points of tangency between the isoquants and the isocost curves.

factor of production　An element (but not an ingredient, as flour is for cake) in production for which there is supply, demand, and a market determined price. Productive factors are traditionally classified as land, labor, and capital, as identified by Adam Smith. We have also included information and financial capital as factors of production. Closely associated with financial capital is liquidity, a more encompassing but more abstract concept.

fungible resources　Resources (commodities) that are identical, (indistinguishable), one from the other. Fungible resources are perfect substitutes, one for the other.

interdealer trading　Dealer-to-dealer trading. Generally motivated by a dealer seeking quickly to rebalance an inventory position.

isocost　A curve that shows how two different factors of production can be combined in different proportions at the same total cost. Each isocost curve is the locus of all of the different labor and capital combinations that require the same level of total expenditure.

isoquant　a curve that shows how two different factors of production can be combined in different proportions that yield equal amounts of output. Each isoquant is the locus of all of the different labor and capital combinations that result in the same level of output. Isoquants in production theory play a similar role as indifferent curves in consumption theory.

long-run average costs　A firm's average cost of output when all inputs are freely variable. Total long-run costs divided by output.

long-run marginal costs　The change in a producer's long-run total cost with respect to a change in its level of output when all factors of production are freely variable (as they are in the long run).

marginal rate of technical substitution　The rate at which a producer can substitute one input for another while keeping output constant. In a two-input environment, the marginal productivity of one input divided by the marginal productivity of the other input. The negative of the slope of an isoquant.

production function　The relationship between the inputs used by a firm and the output of its product.

returns to scale　The rate at which a firm's output increases as inputs are increased proportionately. If equal movements out along a firm's expansion path result in increasing increments of output, the firm is operating with increasing returns to scale; if constant increments of output are realized for equal movements along the path, the firm is operating under conditions of constant returns to scale; and if decreasing increments of output are being realized, the firm is experiencing decreasing returns to scale.

short-run average costs　A firm's average cost of output when, in the short run, one or more factor inputs is fixed. Total short-run cost divided by output.

short-run marginal costs   The increase in a firm's total cost with respect to an increase in output when, in the short run, one or more factor inputs is fixed.

supplemental liquidity   Liquidity that is provided to a market by market makers over and above that which the market would freely supply to itself.

supply curve   A graphic representation of the relationship between the quantity of a product supplied by a firm or an industry, and the price of the product.

systematic risk   *See* nondiversifiable risk.

trading the order flow   Short-term trading by, for example, a market maker or day trader, that is motivated not by fundamental information concerning a stock, but by the stock's dynamic, short-period price behavior. Buying because prices appear to be temporarily depressed, or selling because prices appear to be temporarily elevated, and then trading out of the position once prices have reverted to more appropriate levels.

trading with immediacy   Submitting an order to buy or to sell and receiving an immediate execution. A submitted market order that will trade against a posted limit order or a market maker's quote will generally execute with immediacy.

unbalanced inventory   The accumulation of an unacceptably long position or an unacceptably short position in an asset (e.g., stock or bond).

CURRENT EVENTS DISCUSSIONS

1. Can Markets Be Independent of the Larger Economy, or Are Markets Interdependent?

All markets tend to respond to supplier's costs and customer's demand. At the same time, individual markets also respond to trends and events in markets for related factors of production and substitutes. The following article relates the effects on the steel markets to events in markets for products made from steel, such as automobiles. Also, because steel producers are users of capital, as a factor of production, the steel markets respond to events in the capital markets.

Steelmakers See Demand Fall Sharply, Prices Decline

Steelmakers in the U.S. are experiencing a sharp pullback from buyers who are spooked by the credit crisis and a slowdown in automobile and construction markets, causing inventories to rise and prices on some key products to drop 10%.

Although weakening demand and prices are being partially offset by falling raw-material costs, particularly of scrap, some steelmakers already are cautioning that robust earnings from earlier in the year won't be sustained in the year's second half.

"The instability of financial markets and the general slowdown in the commercial building sector are cause for

concern in coming quarters," said George Stoe, chief operating officer for Worthington Industries Inc., an Ohio-based steel processor.

Demand for rebar steel, often used to build roads, bridges and office buildings, has fallen dramatically in the U.S. because some projects are being delayed or put on hold amid the uncertainty in financial markets, steelmakers said.

Exports for rebar steel fell in July, after six straight months of increases, indicating that demand from foreign markets likely won't be a substitute for weak domestic growth.

The Precision Metalforming Association reported in its latest outlook that more incoming orders from steel fabricators, which shape and form steel for items such as appliances, are expected to drop over the next three months largely because of the uncertainty in the credit markets.

Steel service centers, which act as middlemen between steelmakers and steel end users, also are reporting that their inventories have been ticking steadily upward over the past few months. Steel users are limiting their steel purchases and only buying what they immediately need, fearing that they will be stuck with high-priced steel sitting in their factories.

Hot-rolled steel, a basic building block for most all steel products, is selling for about $1,000 a short ton, off about $110 from earlier this year. That is still relatively high, which should cushion steelmakers' profits.

Many steelmakers are using the slowdown to schedule maintenance outages in hopes that demand will pick up later in the year. ArcelorMittal, the world's biggest steelmaker by production, said that it aims to reduce output by about 15% in certain countries this year. Other steelmakers are likely to follow suit.

Some steelmakers said some markets that consume steel to make pipes and tractors, such as the energy and agriculture sectors, are expected to stay strong.
—**Robert Guy Matthews**, *Wall Street Journal* (September 29, 2008)

Questions

1. With the continuation of the "slump" in automobile sales into 2009 and 2010, what actions would you recommend as the Chief Financial Officer of NUCOR, a major American steel producer? Your CEO needs your recommendations for next Tuesday's meeting of the Executive Committee of the Board at its 9:00 A.M. meeting.

2. Your brother-in-law, a world-famous scrap metal dealer, has told you
that inventories of scrap steel have sharply risen. How will this affect
your recommendations for the Executive Committee?

2. Are Markets Rational or Are They Driven by "Animal Spirits"?

Sometimes markets react violently to "externalities" and the capacities of
market makers. As the liquidity of markets can be largely dependent upon
the capacities of market makers to bear risk and carry inventory, market
prices respond to changes in these capacities. The discussion below recounts
a sharp change in market "sentiment" resulting from an "external" event
that may have reduced the capacities of market makers and the liquidity of
the market.

Stocks Plunge as Rescue Plan Fails to Gain House Approval

*Stocks plunged Monday after the U.S. House of Representatives
voted down a $700 billion rescue plan for Wall Street, leaving the
ailing financial industry and perhaps the broader U.S. economy at
risk.*

*The financial bailout plan failed 206–227 in the House, despite
impassioned debate on the floor and urging for action from President Bush.*

*The Dow Jones Industrial Average plummeted 777.68 points,
or 7%, to 10365.45, hurt by declines in all 30 of its components. It
was the biggest one-day point drop in the 102-year history of the
Dow and the biggest percentage decline since trading resumed after
the 9/11 terror attacks in 2001. The Dow is also down 9.3% since
crisis erupted a few weeks ago on Wall Street following the meltdown of Lehman Brothers Holdings.*

*The bailout's failure throws into limbo the prospects for a fed-
eral intervention that the White House and many financial-industry
veterans believe is necessary to alleviate the burden of soured credit
bets lingering on many banks' books. Those instruments have
clogged Wall Street's usual financing activities for months and, in a
worst-case scenario, could lead to an even more intractable freeze-
up that would deal a severe blow to the broader economy. "There
is a panic mentality afoot today," said Bruce Bittles, chief investment strategist at Robert W. Baird.*

*The S&P 500 plummeted 8.8%, its biggest one-day drop in
percentage terms since the 1987 market crash. The broad measure*

shed 106.59 points to end at 1106.42. All of the S&P's sectors ended lower, led by a 13.2% slide in its financial category. The small-stock Russell 2000 tumbled 6.7%, or 46.94 points, to 657.85. The technology-focused Nasdaq Composite Index fell 9.1%, or 199.61 points, to 1983.73.

The prospect of a bailout package for Wall Street has dominated trading for more than a week, with proponents of an intervention arguing that government action is necessary to keep banks willing and able to extend credit to an array of businesses in other sectors that drive economic growth.

Of course, whether those companies will feel confident enough about the demand outlook for their goods and services to want to expand their operations is a separate matter. Concerns that many companies, at best, will remain on pause in the months ahead hampered stock indexes across the board early in Monday's session.

The lingering risks for investors were underscored as four European institutions sought rescue plans from their local governments and Wachovia became the latest struggling U.S. bank to sell itself off in order to survive.

After the House rejected the proposed rescue plan for Wall Street, the way ahead for investors grew even murkier, traders said.

"We're stunned right now, just trying to figure out what comes next," said one broker at the New York Stock Exchange.

Members of the House took a preliminary vote Monday morning to move the bailout bill forward. But around 1:45 p.m. Washington time, it became clear that the bill would not pass a final vote, prompting a marked pickup in stock selling on the NYSE floor. The final vote was 228–205 against.

As the Congressional vote showed signs of trouble, traders and money managers stared dumbfounded at televisions. Many were angry at Congress's failure to act. "I've been doing this for 45 years and I've never seen anything like this," said Arthur D. Cashin, a trader for UBS on the NYSE floor. "We looked at the vote and went into near free fall. I thought 'We can't be watching this movie.' We thought the adults would show up." Mr. Cashin and other traders were already musing about getting drinks after a hectic day of trading, joking about who would pick up the tab. "There will be a good deal of ice cubes marinating this week," he says. "We're biting our nails down here."

The bailout bill that failed to win passage in the House on Monday was crafted over the weekend by the Bush administration and senior congressional leaders. It called for $250 billion upfront *to be given to the U.S. Treasury to buy troubled assets, which then, subject to Congressional disapproval, could have risen as high as $700 billion. The package now faces an uncertain future, though party leaders on both sides of the aisle are sure to consider revising the legislation, which President Bush said on Monday is needed to "keep the crisis in our financial system from spreading throughout our economy."*

Even on Wall Street, however, the bill had some critics who would've preferred to see a slightly different approach. Traders and analysts widely agreed that some action by the government was necessary, although there were a few dissenters to the idea of having the Treasury buy up distressed credit securities.

Bill King, chief market strategist at M. Ramsey King Securities in Burr Ridge, Ill., said he would've preferred to see the government inject capital into commercial banks and regional firms, cultivating them as successors to failing Wall Street giants as new engines of financing for economic growth.

"There's no question, Wall Street's whole business model is going away," with a heavy emphasis on investment banking and development of ever more complex investment products, said Mr. King.

Investors flocked to U.S. government debt looking for safety on Monday. The yield on the three-month Treasury bill, considered the safest short-term investment, fell to about 0.14% from 0.87% late Friday. The price of the benchmark 10-year note jumped 2-10/32, pushing the yield down to 3.576%, compared to 3.827% late Friday. The troubles in Europe sent the dollar rallying against the euro and the British pound. The U.S. Dollar Index, which measures the greenback's value against a basket of six overseas denominations, rose 0.4%.

Oil futures plunged $10.52, or 9.8%, to $96.37 a barrel in New York as fears about slowing demand due to global economic weakness gripped the commodity markets. The broad Dow Jones-AIG Commodity Index slid 5.2%.

Analysts said the flurry of developments around the world is confirming fears that the global financial contagion is likely to spread further before any recovery. "There's an increasing realization that the cleanup and the mending of all that's gone wrong is going to take an extended period to work through, and we're going to see an extended recovery period," said Jamie Spiteri, senior dealer at Shaw Stockbroking in Sydney.

—**Peter A. McKay,** *Wall Street Journal* (**September 30, 2008**)

Questions

1. For a class discussion, prepare a set of recommendations for the reduction of volatility in the equities markets that gives consideration to the following factors.
   - Increasing the capital requirements for membership in the New York Stock Exchange.
   - Changing the inventory requirements of brokers and dealers so that all brokers and all dealers must carry minimum inventories.
   - Precluding dealers from trading directly with other dealers; that is, they may trade only with investors.

2. As the newly appointed head of the Securities and Exchange Commission's Market Regulation Division, you have been assigned the task of increasing the liquidity of both the New York Stock Exchange and the NASDAQ. The commission will be meeting tomorrow morning and they wish to publish new regulations immediately that will achieve this objective. What recommendations will you present to the commission?

REVIEW QUESTIONS

1. Which of the following is TRUE at the point where an isocost line is tangent to an isoquant?
   a. $P_{Labor}/P_{Capital} = MRTS_{Labor.Capital}$.
   b. $P_{Labor}/P_{Capital} = MRS_{X.Y}$.
   c. $P_X/P_Y = MRTS_{Labor.Capital}$.
   d. None of the above.

2. Which of the following is FALSE about the total cost curve?
   a. As output increases, constant returns to scale are followed by increasing returns to scale and then by decreasing returns to scale.
   b. Total cost curve is increasing throughout.
   c. Increasing returns to scale are expected at low levels of output and decreasing returns to scale are expected at high levels of output.
   d. Diseconomies of scale set in at high levels of output because coordinating the production process becomes more difficult.

3. Which of the following is correct about the expansion path?
   a. The slope of an expansion path is affected by technology, because technology determines the slope of the isoquant curves.
   b. The slope of an expansion path is affected by the price of labor relative to price capital, because the price relative determines the slope of the isocost lines.

    c. Expansion path is a locus of all tangency points between firm's iso-cost lines and isoquant curves.

    d. All of the above are correct.

4. Which of the following statements about the relationship between the long-run MC and AC curves is FALSE?

    a. The MC curve crosses the AC curve at the point of the AC curve's minimum.

    b. The AC curve crosses the MC curve at the point of the MC curve's minimum.

    c. The MC curve lies below the AC curve in the area where the AC curve is decreasing.

    d. The MC curve lies above the AC curve in the area where the AC curve is increasing.

5. Which of the following represents a cost associated with market making operations?

    a. The cost of holding an unbalanced inventory, that is, being exposed to diversifiable risk.

    b. The cost of commitment, that is, having to trade with anyone who wants to sell or buy shares.

    c. The cost of ignorance, that is, the possibility of transacting with a momentum trader.

    d. None of the above.

6. With reference to a total cost curve, the average cost at a given level of output, X, can be represented as

    a. The slope of the line that is tangent to the TC curve at X.

    b. The slope of the ray from the origin to the point on the TC curve at X.

    c. The height of the TC curve at X.

    d. None of the above.

7. With economies of scale that are external to individual firms but are internal to their industry, which of the following is TRUE?

    a. The supply curve of the industry is more elastic than it otherwise would be because of the existence of these scale economies.

    b. The supply curve of the industry can be downward sloping.

    c. The height of the MC and AC curves for an individual firm falls as an industry output increases, all else equal.

    d. All of the above.

8. The supply curve for a firm in a competitive industry is

    a. Its AC curve in the region to the right of its minimum point.

    b. Its MC curve in the region to the right of its minimum point.

    c. Its MC curve in the region where marginal costs are equal to or are greater than average costs.

    d. Its marginal revenue curve in its entirety.

9. A firm's supply curve is well defined when
    a. The demand curve facing the firm is downward sloping.
    b. The demand curve facing the firm is infinitely elastic.
    c. The firm is big enough to have the power to set its own price.
    d. Both **b** and **c**.

10. The best profit output for a competitive firm is determined by
    a. Any point where $MC = MR$.
    b. The point where $MC = MR$ and $MC > AC$.
    c. The point where $MC = MR$ and $AC > MC$.
    d. The point where $AC = MR$ and $MC > AC$.

11. The market maker is a
    a. Sell-side intermediary who participates in trading as a principal.
    b. Sell-side intermediary who acts as an agent/broker.
    c. Buy-side intermediary who participates in trading as a principal.
    d. Buy-side intermediary who acts as an agent/broker.

12. Which of the following actions can be used by a dealer firm to appropriately control its inventory?
    a. Raise its bid when it has an unacceptably large long position.
    b. Lower its offer when it has an unacceptably large short position.
    c. Work off its inventory imbalance by trading with another dealer.
    d. All of the above.

13. The key service provided by the market maker is
    a. Accessibility.
    b. Velocity.
    c. Immediacy.
    d. Periodicity.

14. The formula that determines the maximum amount of output that can be produced with K units of capital and L units of labor is the
    a. Production function.
    b. Technological constraint.
    c. Research and development schedule.
    d. Total product.

15. Which of the following is TRUE when a firm minimizes its total expenditures for a given level of output?
    a. The $MRTS$ is equal to the ratio of input prices.
    b. The marginal products per dollar spent on all inputs are equal.
    c. The marginal products of all inputs are equal.
    d. The $MRTS$ is equal to the ratio of input prices and the marginal products per dollar spent on all inputs is equal.

16. The combinations of inputs that produce a given level of output are depicted by

   a. Indifference curves.

   b. Budget lines.

   c. Isocost lines.

   d. Isoquant curves.

17. Changes in the price of an input cause

   a. Isoquants to become steeper.

   b. Parallel shifts of the isocost lines.

   c. Slope changes in the isocost lines.

   d. Parallel shifts of the isoquant curves.

18. The marginal product of an input is defined as the change in

   a. Average output attributable to the last unit of an input.

   b. Total output attributable to the last unit of an input.

   c. Total input attributable to the last unit of an output.

   d. Average output attributable to the last unit of an output.

19. The marginal rate of technical substitution

   a. Determines the rate at which a producer can substitute between two inputs in order to produce one additional unit of output.

   b. Is constant along the isoquant curve.

   c. Is the absolute value of the slope of the isoquant.

   d. Is the absolute value of marginal revenue.

20. Two identical firms may merge because of the existence of

   a. Economies of scope.

   b. Economies of scale.

   c. Both **a** and **b**.

   d. None of the above is correct.

APPLICATIONS AND ISSUES

The Optimal Schooling Behavior of Fish

We have devoted considerable attention in this chapter to understanding the supply behavior of firms in a perfectly competitive industry. You might question the extent to which actual firms in real-world, competitive industries behave in accordance with our model. Of course the owners of the firms respond to economic variables. Of course they will strive to bring more to market when market prices are higher and/or when input prices are lower. But do they really know their cost curves? Do they really *maximize* their profits?

Of course not. Information is never perfect enough for anyone to be able to do this, and decision making is never sharp enough to deliver perfect-world answers. But, as we pointed out in Chapter 2, our microeconomic models do not claim to describe the behavior of every economic agent. Rather, they seek to predict what the representative household or firm will do (a positive as distinct from a normative application). We describe the central tendency of a group and, in so doing, are actually modeling the behavior of the group as an aggregate. An intriguing question to ask in light of all of this is how much explicit rational thinking is actually required on the part of individual decision makers for our predictions of group behavior to be reasonably accurate? This inquiry is what our thought question for this chapter is all about.

Let's consider a species that is not known for having much grey matter—fish. An interesting thing about many types of fish is their schooling behavior. There are benefits to schooling. It is believed that schooling may reduce friction and so enable energy to be conserved when the fish are on the move. There can be safety in numbers as some foolish predators may think that 75 little fish, all packed tightly together, are actually one big fish. There is a confusion factor: The mass behavior of a sizable school can confuse a predator (think of the difficulty that some of us have catching just one ball when two or more balls are thrown at us at the same time).

Schooling also allows individual fish to communicate rapidly with one another. Have you ever observed a school of little fish? Have you noticed how, with lightning speed, the school can change course and set off in a new direction? Eyesight and highly sensitive lateral lines on the fishes' bodies enable them to do this. Here is the picture: A predator suddenly appears, and the fish closest to the predator detect the danger, change direction, and rapidly dart away. Knowledge of this maneuver is transmitted virtually instantly throughout the entire school which, as a group (perhaps minus one or two) dashes away.

Animal scientists have asked the question "Why do fish school?" and they have advanced testable hypotheses such as those we have just presented. An economist will ask another question or two. Is there an *optimal* configuration for a school? Why might the optimal configuration be different for different types of fish? And there is the classic economic question: Are there trade-offs involved that would enable us to model the optimal configuration of a school for a given kind of fish? With these economist-type questions in mind, we ask you to work your way through the following thoughts and questions:

1. Using methodology that you are now familiar with (and may appreciate for the simplicity that it delivers), introduce a trade-off situation in a two factor model. To start, we can pick one of the benefits of schooling that we have just identified. Let's select the transmission of information factor, and assume that information can be transmitted more quickly

from fish to fish if they are schooled more tightly together. Now, to have a trade-off situation, something must be given up if the school is tighter. That is why a second factor is needed. Can you think of a suitable second factor?

2. Here is a suggestion for the second factor: A school of fish moving though a food field will be able to consume more food per fish when the fish are less tightly grouped together. So, there you have it. The trade-off is between protection from predators (which is greater the shorter the distance between the fish), and per fish consumption (which is greater the greater is the distance between them). We ask you to plot this trade-off. So that we can be consistent, put protection (P) on the vertical axis and consumption (C) on the horizontal axis.

3. Hopefully you have made your line downward sloping (after all, we are dealing with a trade-off). The line plays the role of a technologically determined efficient frontier (a kind of budget constraint). Our question now is, what must change for there to be a movement along the curve? That is, what variable, by changing, will move the fish from one point on the frontier to another?

4. Okay, question 3 was fairly easy. The distance between the fish is the variable that we were asking about. When the school is more spread out it realizes more C and less P, and when it is packed more tightly together it enjoys more P and less C. So let's proceed to a more challenging question. Is the efficient frontier linear or curved? If curved, is it concave or convex from below?

5. The answer to number 4 depends on the marginal productivity of the distance between the fish in delivering P and C. Call the variable "distance." Assume that increasing distance has diminishing productivity in terms of delivering C. Further assume that decreasing distance has diminishing productivity in terms of delivering P. Now answer the question in number 4.

6. With the efficient frontier (a.k.a., the technologically determined budget constraint) identified, how is an optimal point along it found? By, of course, interfacing the frontier with a family of indifference curves. Accordingly, we ask you to add a family of indifference curves to your graph. But do not simply draw these curves in by rote. Make sure that their curvature makes sense to you.

7. Can the model be extended to suggest why optimal schooling behavior is different for different kinds of fish? Can we formulate some comparative statics? Of course we can. We ask you to give it a try. Contrast the optimal solution for two schools of fish, A and B, with the fish in school A being smaller than the fish in school B. Assume that, in the limit, for both schools, as the distance between the fish becomes infinitesimally

small, protection reaches the same maximum (P^{MAX}). As the distance between the fish increases, consumption (C) increases for both schools, but assume that this too reaches a limit. Let the limit value of C be greater for the larger fish than it is for the smaller fish ($C^{MAX(A)} < C^{MAX(B)}$). Now introduce their indifference curves and contrast the resulting equilibrium solutions. Which type of fish does your model suggest will school more closely together, A or B?

8. We started this thought question by asking how much explicitly rational thinking is required on the part of individual participants, in any kind of market, for our predictions of group behavior to be reasonably accurate. What do you think? Do fish behave as if they know all of the things that you have just figured out? And here is one final question: Do fish really have indifference curves?

Controlling Costs and Overcoming Inefficiency

Costs for producers are the major focus of management. Management has less real control of customer demand for their product, with marketing and advertising being an additional cost of speculative efficacy. Therefore management exercises its determined efforts to develop and employ strategies to lower unit costs. In competitive markets, the producer who can bring its product to the market at the lowest cost has a distinct advantage in pricing flexibility and potential profit. The optimal combination of the factors of production in obtaining minimal unit cost is the production function of management.

The tabular display shown next is of the "law of diminishing returns" or "decreasing returns to scale." It assumes a single factor of production, labor, in the making of our product X. Yet any other factors of production (capital, technology, or land) might be used in this table. The productivity declines as increasing units of labor are employed, from 13 units of X from the first worker to a mere 2 units of X from the sixth worker. Confounding the cost problem is the increasing average cost of workers as the less skilled, more disruptive, and less amenable are employed. Part of the per-worker cost increase is the growing need for supervision, accounting, and administration (sometimes referred to as labor administration) as the work force expands. Two market alternatives are presented: the pricing of X at either 25 cents or 50 cents. Yet in both cases the "law" retains its effect.

Question

The question to be considered is what actions can be taken to ameliorate the relentless, remorseless, and seeming irremediable growth of costs.

The Marginal-Cost Curve and the Firm's Supply Decision (in this case, the "control variable" is an additional laborer's production)

Laborer # (@)	Total Product X	Wage Rate	Margin Product Cost	Total Cost	Revenue @25c	Revenue @50c	Profits @25c	Profits @50c
0	0	0	0	0	0	0	0	0
1(13)	13	$1.00	.076	$1.00	$3.25	6.50	$2.25	5.50
2(12)	25	2.00	.167	4.00	6.25	12.50	2.25	8.50
3(9)	34	3.00	.222	9.00	8.50	17.00	(.50)	8.00
4(7)	41	4.00	.571	16.00	10.25	20.50	(4.75)	4.50
5(5)	46	5.00	1.00	25.00	11.50	23.00	(13.50)	(2.00)
6(2)	48	6.00	3.00	36.00	12.00	24.00	(24.00)	(12.00)

Management Strategies to Optimize Efficiency

In the year 1870 the entrepreneur J. Davison Rockefeller began the expansion of his enterprise, later named Standard Oil (today known as EXXON) in the illuminating oil business. The source of his raw material for production was the crude oil (petroleum) being extracted from the oil fields of western Pennsylvania and eastern Ohio. The refinement of the crude oil was done by a simple process of distillation. The product was sold to middlemen who in turn shipped and distributed it to customers. The record reflected a pattern of constantly rising marginal costs for labor materials and capital.

The refining business, which was centered in Cleveland, Ohio, was highly competitive, with many producers. The "wildcatters" drilling for the petroleum were flooding the market with crude oil in a volatile price environment. The cost of labor was high, capital was not readily attracted to this chaotic industry, and profits were substantial but fleeting. It appeared that this situation was driven by the remorseless laws of diminishing returns with industry profits being reduced to elimination.

Rockefeller over the next 30 years sought to bring "order" to this chaotic market, and his success in countering the relentless laws of diminishing returns through strategies of technological innovation, production-distribution integration, and economies of scale produced one of the largest personal fortunes in American history. The next table reflects his attack on the cost structure of his firm in the 30 years after 1870.

Standard Oil and the Economies of Scale (costs per gallon in a market of "elastic demand")

	1870	1900
1. Petroleum production (crude oil)	5 cents	2 cents
2. Refining	8 cents	4 cents
3. Distribution (rail, pipeline, ships)	5 cents	2 cents
4. Marketing and sales	5 cents	1 cent
5. General and administration	1 cents	2 cents
Total Costs	*24 cents*	*11 cents*
6. Profit @ 15%	3 cents	2 cents
7. Sales price	27 cents	13 cents

Question

Consider these circumstances and be prepared to discuss the consequential competitive position of Standard Oil in 1900.

ADDITIONAL READINGS

Friedman, Thomas L. *The World Is Flat.* New York: Farrar, Straus and Giroux, 2005.

>The *New York Times*'s commentator on the evolution of the knowledge economy and its globalization.

Mokyr, Joel. *The Gifts of Athena: Origins of the Knowledge Economy.* Princeton, NJ: Princeton University Press, 2002.

>An original analytic framework to the concept of useful knowledge and its effects upon social networks and markets in the evolution of the knowledge economy.

ANSWERS TO REVIEW QUESTIONS

1. a
2. a
3. d
4. b
5. a
6. b
7. d
8. c
9. b
10. b
11. a
12. c
13. c
14. a
15. d
16. d
17. c
18. b
19. c
20. b

Sources and Nature of Competition

LEARNING OBJECTIVES

■ **Understand the important role that price plays as a competitive variable.** Price is of major importance as a competitive variable because the structure of relative prices directly affects the production and consumption decisions of firms and households. Firms respond to price depending on the competitive structure of the industry that they are in (perfect competition, monopoly, monopsonistic competition, or oligopoly). Comprehending just how this works is a major objective of Chapter 6.

■ **Understand the importance of nonprice competition.** In many settings, nonprice competition (via, for instance, product quality, product innovation, advertising, delivery, and servicing) can distinguish a firm, strengthen its position in the marketplace, and contribute to profits.

■ **Be familiar with the nature of perfect competition.** A perfectly competitive market is one where the product produced is a fungible generic, and where every participant is sufficiently small relative to the aggregate so that no individual buyer or seller has the power to affect the product's price. Under perfect competition in a free market environment, price is set by the intersection of supply and demand. You should understand the no-profit, long-run competitive equilibrium solution, the difference between economic profits and economic rents, the condition under which the long-run supply curve of a competitive industry is infinitely elastic, and the role that consumer surplus, producer surplus, and deadweight loss play in all of this.

■ **Be familiar with the nature of monopoly.** For a monopoly, just one firm comprises the industry. As such, the firm faces no direct competition, and the demand curve for its product is downward sloping. Be sensitive to the fact, however, that the monopoly firm does face competition from all other items in consumers' shopping baskets. You should understand how the monopoly firm sets its best profit price and output, how this price, quantity equilibrium differs from the solution for a perfectly competitive industry, why a monopoly equilibrium is inefficient from a static analytical perspective, and how a socially desirable equilibrium price and output can be attained (if a regulatory agency has sufficient information). One further thing should be understood, the very existence of monopolies. To address this one, the chapter introduces you to two concepts, *barriers to entry* and *natural monopoly*. A market tactic of producers and distributors is to distinguish their products as having recognizable superiority (such as Heinz's ketchup, Skippy's peanut butter, and Tiffany's "little blue box"). Branding products discourages competitors from entering an industry with new and competing products.

■ **Be comfortable with the terms *economies of scale* and *economies of scope*.** The achievement of production efficiencies through continuous reductions of average unit cost permits a supplier to bring its products and services to market at competitively favorable prices. As an economy of scope, the achievement of, for instance, distribution efficiencies also bestows pricing advantages in distribution. Economies of scale and of scope can inhibit competition and, if they extend over large enough ranges of output, can lead to a natural monopoly.

■ **Be familiar with imperfect competition.** Between perfect competition on one end of the spectrum and monopoly on the other, there lies a broad spectrum of industry structures that are called *imperfectly competitive*. Here, the firms do compete with one another, but the demand curve facing each firm is not infinitely elastic. Two broad classifications are used for these industry types: monopolistic competition and oligopoly.

■ **Be familiar with monopolistic competition.** You should recognize the distinctive characteristics of monopolistic competition: There are many firms in the industry (enough so that competition eliminates profits in the long run), but the product produced is not a fungible generic. Instead, each firm faces a downward-sloping (albeit highly elastic) demand curve for its product, because it retains a "monopoly" position with regard to a unique feature(s) of its product.

■ **Be familiar with oligopolistic competition.** The distinctive feature of oligopolistic competition is that the number of firms in the industry is small enough for the firms to compete directly with one another. Each firm, in making its own competitive decisions, takes into account the *competitive reactions* of the other firms in the industry. You should appreciate what these competitive reactions entail, and the important role that nonprice competition plays for the oligopoly firms.

■ **Appreciate how competition plays out in an equity market.** Two issues of major importance are addressed: first, the reluctance of large traders to disclose their orders and the attending book-building problem, and second, the dynamics of interdealer competition in a quote-driven market. You should know how a monopoly/monopsony model can be applied to determine equilibrium for a market with just one market maker. Regarding the competitive dealer market, you should gain a richer appreciation of how different dealer firms compete with each other, and the limited nature of the control that they have over the price of their service.

■ **Achieve a more comprehensive sense of the importance of price as a competitive variable.** The chapter ends with a discussion of a most important issue: the importance of price as a competitive variable. Producer and distributor firms' profitability is largely determined by their efficiencies in controlling costs, and a structure of input prices underlies their costs. But very critically, their ability to set and reset the prices of their products and services determines their effectiveness as competitors, and their success in achieving the goal of gaining market share and realizing economies of scale and of scope.

CHAPTER SUMMARY

Robust competition is the force that economists rely on to discipline the micro markets, to drive the markets to greater efficiency, to deliver product innovation, and to keep markets growing. How does competition play out? What are the key competitive variables? How does competitive behavior depend on the structure of an industry? These are among the questions that we have addressed in this chapter. Here are the 18 highlights:

1. We first considered the perfectly competitive environment. Under perfect competition, all firms produce an identical (fungible) product and the number of firms is big enough so that no one firm is large enough to have any discernable influence on aggregate market outcomes. In the perfectly competitive industry, all firms are atomistic.

2. So, how do perfectly competitive firms compete? Not in the ways that we typically think that firms fight it out in the marketplace. Rather, these firms collectively put pressure on each other via the effect that their aggregate output has on price. *Ceteris paribus*, higher prices lead to profits, profits attract new entrants into an industry, and the larger aggregate output that follows puts downward pressure on price until the excess returns are eliminated. Conversely, lower prices lead to losses

that force firms out of an industry. In general, competition drives each firm to produce efficiently (i.e., to operate at a least cost combination of inputs and at a best profit output level of production).

3. In long-run equilibrium, firms in a perfectly competitive industry do not make economic profits. If all firms in an industry are identical (that is, have identical production functions and cost curves), they each realize just enough total revenue to cover their costs of doing business. If the firms are not identical, those that are intramarginal (the firms with lower average cost curves) do realize excess returns, but these returns are called economic rents, not profits.

4. Frictionless, long-run equilibrium has excellent economic properties for a perfectly competitive industry. Under perfect competition, price and industry output are determined by the intersection of the industry's aggregate demand and supply curves. Price (which, we have seen in Chapter 2, is related to marginal utility) is equated with marginal cost, and both producer and consumer surplus are maximized. When the free and frictionless market equilibrium is perturbed by, for instance, the imposition of a sales tax, the industry's producers and consumers in aggregate incur a deadweight loss.

5. If perfect competition is on one end of the spectrum, monopoly is on the other. With perfect competition an unlimited number of firms are in the industry; with monopoly, the industry has just one firm. For both the perfectly competitive industry and the monopolized industry, we have very clear models of how price and output are determined in a frictionless, deterministic (rather than stochastic), and static (rather than dynamic) environment.

6. Before an industry can be classified as being monopolized, the product under question (and therefore the industry) has to be defined. Is the product tubular steel, or is it steel in general, or is it all structural building materials? The answer depends on the cross elasticities of demand. If the cross elasticities are low for a particular kind of steel, then that particular kind of steel can be taken to be "the product," and if there is only one firm producing it, then that firm would be a monopolist. If the cross elasticities are high, then close substitutes exist and the product should be defined more broadly. Perhaps more than one firm is producing the more broadly defined product, in which case the single firm that is producing the specialized steel had best not be thought of as a monopolist.

7. Like the perfectly competitive firm, the monopolistic firm maximizes its profits by producing at an output level that equates marginal revenue and marginal cost. But unlike the perfectly competitive firm, the demand curve facing the monopoly is the demand curve facing the

industry, and the industry demand curve is downward sloping (that is, it is not infinitely elastic). In this case, marginal revenue is less than price, which means that the monopoly firm does not equate price with marginal cost. Rather, price is higher and output is less. This comparative static is undesirable from a public policy perspective. We have noted that "keep the markets competitive" is a mantra for many economists and government regulators.

8. Several things were concluded about the monopoly firm. (1) It does not have a supply curve—the very terminology does not apply (although its price and output are nevertheless determinant); (2) The monopoly firm will always operate in the elastic part of its demand curve (for the competitive industry, equilibrium is wherever demand crosses supply, and nothing prevents the crossing point from being in the inelastic portion of the industry demand curve); and (3) A monopolistic firm, if it is able to segment its market, can increase profits by price discrimination (selling less and charging a higher price in a less elastic segment, and selling more and charging a lower price in a more elastic segment).

9. If monopolies are undesirable (at least in a static environment), why do they exist? The answer is three words long: "barriers to entry." Product innovation, patents, copyright protection, well-kept secrets, and a government license or a franchise are important barriers.

10. Another particularly effective barrier to entry is economies of scale. A market is said to be a *natural monopoly* when with scale economies a firm's average cost curve is falling over output ranges that are large relative to the market's aggregate demand for the firm's product. We also considered two related concepts, economies of scope and network externalities.

11. Having completed our discussion of the two ends of the spectrum of market structures, we turned to the vast majority of firms that operate somewhere in between them, in a rather grey environment called *imperfect competition*. Perfectly competitive firms cannot affect the prices of the products that they produce, and thus they do not set price. With imperfect competition and monopoly, the firm does set the price of its product. Thus it is an *administered price*. As we have noted, we do a good job modeling the price administered by a monopolist. But the models of imperfect competition are not as definitive, and we have a number of different formulations. That is why we just called the environment "grey."

12. The first case of imperfect competition that we dealt with is *monopolistic competition*. A substantial number of firms can operate in a monopolistically competitive industry but, unlike under perfect competition, the products that they produce are to some extent differentiated.

Accordingly, the demand curve facing each firm in a monopolistically competitive industry is downward sloping. But because there are many firms in the industry (there are no serious barriers to entry), competition eliminates profits for each of the firms, much as it does for perfectly competitive firms.

Profits are eliminated because their receipt attracts new entrants into an industry. As new firms enter, the demand curves facing the existing firms shift down and to the left until, for the marginal firm, its demand curve is tangent to its average cost curve. Because the demand curve is downward sloping, the average cost curve is necessarily downward sloping at the point of tangency, and thus the marginal firm's average cost is not minimized, as it would be under perfect competition. We viewed the higher average cost under monopolistic competition as a price that is paid by consumers because they are willing to pay for variety, because they accept paying for the product differences that distinguish monopolistic competition from perfect competition.

13. The other case of imperfect competition is *oligopolistic competition*. Whether the firms in such an industry produce a differentiated product or a fungible product does not matter. The distinguishing feature of oligopolistic competition is that the firms are few enough in number so that each reacts to the strategic decisions of the others. Very importantly, knowing this, each firm takes its competitors' reactions into account when making its own strategic decisions. Let's put it this way: One reality alone characterizes competition in an oligopolistic industry—the firms take into account the interplay between their own competitive decisions and the responses of their competitors.

14. We presented a standard oligopoly pricing formulation that delivers an interesting economic explanation of why administered prices are relatively constant over time (as they are generally observed to be in an oligopolistic industry): the *kinked demand curve model*. The model is based on two different competitive responses: (1) A firm's price increases are not followed, but (2) its price cuts are matched. This asymmetric response puts the kink in the demand curve, the kink translates into a discontinuity in the marginal revenue curve, and the discontinuity accounts for the relative stability of price (the MC curve can shift up and down through the discontinuous part of the MR curve, and the demand curve can shift to the right and the left without changing the best profit output).

15. We next turned to a duopoly (two competing firms) and to the equilibrium formulation of the Nobel laureate John Nash. Nash's game theoretic model is structured with regard to competitive strategies in general, and it can be applied not only to the firms' pricing policies, but

also to their other competitive decisions (for instance, their marketing and product differentiation strategies). The key insight delivered by Nash equilibrium is that although the duopoly firms may each be following a self-optimizing strategy, both firms attain an equilibrium position that is not as desirable as the outcome they could have attained if they had acted cooperatively.

16. With the oligopoly discussion in hand, we switched gears and considered how competition plays out in the equity markets. To this end, we first applied the Nash model to a setting where two large equity traders (a buyer and a seller) are deciding whether to enter their big orders in an opening call auction or in a continuous market that follows. True to Nash equilibrium, our two players both did something that is mutually undesirable: they both avoided the call auction and waited for the continuous market.

17. Continuing with our focus on the dealer market, we gave an overview of market maker operations, presented a monopoly/monopsony dealer pricing model, and described some of the intricacies of interdealer competition in an oligopolistic market maker environment. Competition in this equity market clearly is complex and multifaceted.

18. The chapter concluded with a discussion of the importance of price as a competitive variable. Quite clearly, although price is of critical importance, it is not the only competitive variable in the micro markets. We provided a taste of what competition involves in the equity markets. A more general question is how much can we rely on competition to provide the desired carrots and sticks that keep us, as a society, on the path of robust economic growth and performance? These two issues concerning the efficiency of the marketplace and the efficiency of government regulatory intervention are dealt with in the remaining two chapters of the book.

GLOSSARY

administered prices Prices set by firms that have the market power to do so.

asynchronous order flow The staggered sequence in which buy and sell orders arrive in the market. In other words, buy and sell orders do not arrive at the market at the same time.

barriers to entry Anything that precludes a new seller from entering a market. For example, a government license, patent protection, control over a scare resource, and substantial economies of scale are barriers.

book building We use the term in this book to describe the process of buy and sell orders being placed on a limit order book so that the book will become deeper (offer more liquidity). Book building in the secondary equity markets is particularly important at the start of each trading day. The term is more commonly used in relation to building investor interest in a stock at the time of its initial pubic offering (IPO).

consumer surplus   The (larger) total amount that a purchaser (consumer) would be willing to pay for X units of a good (the purchaser's reservation price times X) less the (smaller) total amount that has to be paid (the market price for X times X), because the market price of X is less than the purchaser's reservation price for X.

contestable markets   Markets that face the threat of competition from potential new entrants.

deadweight loss   The reduction of total economic surplus (consumer surplus plus producer surplus) when output is less than the frictionless, free-market equilibrium output, and price is higher for buyers and/or lower for sellers.

duopoly   A market in which there are just two firms competing with each other.

economic rent   Excess returns ($TR - TC > 0$) to a firm that cannot be competed away in the long run by other firms entering the industry. Returns (for a firm) that are attributable to a special advantage that the firm enjoys (such as may be offered by its location). Rents are differentiated from economic profits, which can be competed away in the long run.

economies of scale   Economies achieved by a firm by producing a larger output. The relationship between long-run average cost and output. A firm's long-run average cost curve is decreasing over the range of output for which it is experiencing economies of scale. Long-run average costs are constant under constant returns to scale, and are rising under diseconomies of scale.

economies of scope   Economies achieved by a firm from the production and distribution of multiple products. Economies of scope are differentiated from economies of scale.

imperfect competition   Characterizes a market that is neither perfectly competitive nor monopolized. Monopolistic competition and oligopolistic competition.

inside spread   The inside market. The difference between the lowest of all of the ask quotes and the highest of all of the bid quotes.

kinked demand curve model   A model of oligopolistic competition. The model implies that administered prices will be relatively constant in an oligopoly industry (as they are observed to be).

monopolistic competition   Characterizes markets where barriers to entry are low, and enough firms are in the industry so that no two firms will strategically respond to each others' pricing and output decisions. The outputs of the competing firms are somewhat differentiated under monopolistic competition (while they are fungible under perfect competition).

monopoly   An industry where one firm is the sole producer/supplier of the product.

monopsony   An industry where one firm is the sole buyer of the product.

Nash equilibrium   In a gaming situation, an equilibrium that is reached by a small number of contestants who, because they do not cooperate with each other, fail to achieve the larger positive payouts (or lesser negative payouts) that would have been attainable if they had cooperated. A formulation that is applied (among other things) to oligopolistically competitive firms. The model was set forth by the Nobel laureate John Nash.

network externalities   When the users of a product can be viewed as having formed a network, and where the value of the network for the users increases with the number of members in the network. No one participant, in deciding whether to join a network, takes into account the value that his or her joining would have for others, which accounts for the use of the term "externality." Fax machines are a good example of a network (the more people who have a fax machine, the more people anyone with such a machine can send a fax to), but nobody while buying a fax machine takes account of the benefit that his or her purchase will bestow on others.

oligopoly   An industry that comprises a few enough number of firms for the firms in that industry to respond to each other's competitive decisions (e.g., pricing product innovation and advertising decisions).

perfect competition   A market that meets the following conditions: (1) The product produced by the industry is across all firms identical (fungible), (2) many buyers and sellers are in the industry, and (3) no long-run barriers to entry or exit. Each firm in a perfectly competitive industry is "atomistic." Being atomistic, no individual firm in a perfectly competitive industry has any power to affect the price of the product that defines the industry.

preferencing   A common practice in equity trading that refers to an order being sent to (preferenced to) a specific dealer (or market) regardless of the price that is being quoted by other dealers (or markets). Preferencing occurs because of a special relationship or arrangement with that dealer (or market). The dealer firm to whom an order has been preferenced will typically match the best quote currently posted on the market.

price discrimination   A firm's practice of segmenting its market and selling the same product to different customers at different prices. Relatively high prices are charged in market segments where demand is relatively price inelastic, and relatively low prices are charged in market segments where demand is relatively price elastic.

price improvement   Providing a customer with a better price than the price that has been publicly quoted. Executing a market buy order at a price lower than the lowest quoted offer, and executing a market sell order at a price higher than the highest quoted bid.

price priority   The most aggressively priced order (the highest bid or the lowest ask) executes first.

prisoners' dilemma   A special case of a competitive (typically two-party) game that results in a Nash equilibrium. So-called because it represents the strategic behavior of two individuals who, having been apprehended for a crime, are being interrogated by the police in separate rooms (so that the prisoners cannot coordinate their stories).

producer surplus   The (larger) total amount that a producer (supplier) receives for selling X units of output less the (smaller) total amount that the producer (supplier) would have been willing to receive. Producer surplus is realized when the market price of X is greater than the producer's reservation price for supplying X.

quote matching   Upon receiving a preferenced order from a customer, a dealer firm will generally execute the customer's order at the current best quote in the market (highest bid or lowest offer), regardless of what the dealer firm may itself have been quoting at the time it received the order.

tick size   The minimum price variation. The units in which prices are stated (e.g., pennies).

time priority   A rule of trading which specifies that if two or more orders are tied at the most aggressive price, the order that has been placed first will execute first.

CURRENT EVENTS DISCUSSIONS

1. Does Competition Exist between Markets?

Markets respond to competition from many sources, as well as their internal traditions and architecture. In addition, the externalities of their environments and the cross price elasticities of their costs affect their efficiencies. The two articles below deal with two markets with different competitive structures. In both cases, the distribution of the product (equities transactions and home appliances) are being effected by competitive pressures and technological change. The first article, from the London *Economist*, discusses the forces that bear on the future of one of the world's oldest and largest equities markets.

The City of London: Defying Augury

Can the stock exchange and the City see off the competition?

As the British economy heads straight for the doldrums, the City is struggling too. Recent moves by the London Stock Exchange designed to see off encroaching rivals may cost the LSE custom rather than increase it. And even if the 300-year-old market can change its ways, the financial centre it buttresses may well be shaky. The signs are not good.

This week the LSE slashed its trading fees to match those of electronic trading platforms (known as MTFs), and said it would allow ultra-fast computerised traders to put their machines close to the LSE's own computers. This will save the increasingly important program traders precious nanoseconds between sending an order and executing the trade. In July the stock exchange struck a deal with Lehman Brothers, an investment bank, to form Baikal, a so-called "dark pool" that allows high-volume trades to be executed bit-by-bit off-exchange and out of the public eye—that is, in competition with the LSE itself. The LSE still has a near-monopoly in listing stocks and providing price data, but increasing volumes are being traded on electronic platforms. Chi-X, launched last year, already has 15% of London's share-trading volume. Other rivals are queuing up.

The LSE may be able to shrug off such virtual-market upstarts but it has yet to figure out how to expand its business as Europe's flagship exchange. AIM, its market for international and domestic start-up companies, is shrinking for the first time. And the LSE's merger last year with the Italian Stock Exchange has proved a disaster.

Its woes are symptomatic of waxing disenchantment with London as a financial centre. City types say the brightest and richest are moving to other parts, particularly Asia. London is uncomfortable and expensive. A £30,000 ($53,000) flat tax on foreign residents and a rise in capital-gains tax has hit the whizz kids in the pocket. Lay-offs at shrinking banks—35,000 have been announced and up to 100,000 are expected—have depressed job and bonus prospects. The golden days, when adding complexity to financial products brought immediate reward, are over.

Then there is London's reputation as a place to do business. The handling of Northern Rock, a troubled mortgage lender, revealed regulators with feet of clay. City lobbyists are fighting cumbersome backdoor financial meddling from Brussels. The City of London's global financial-centres index—which in March put London and New York well ahead of other centres, though losing ground—will probably show that the gap has narrowed further when new results come out this month.

Should London care? The 2012 Olympics will provide displacement activity; London's other invisible-export earners—shipping, insurance, commodities, professional services—seem unaffected. But the shrinking of wholesale financial markets could have a direct impact on the skyline.

—The Economist (September 4, 2008)

In some markets the price competition is affected by a variety of singular practices and the oversight of the courts. Home appliance markets are driven by both new home construction as well as replacements.

Fixed Prices May Be Back, But Who Are They Helping?

After last year's Supreme Court ruling ("Price-Fixing Makes Comeback After Supreme Court Ruling," page one, Aug. 18), high-end appliance makers, such as SubZero and Viking, instructed regional distributors to experiment with unilateral minimum resale price

(UMRP) policies. In a perfect world, I agree with UMRP policies, but I think the implementation of this UMRP is ill-timed, said a SubZero spokewoman.

In a weak housing market, where all appliance sales are off at least 20% and there is a saturation of dealers in the area, the competition for customers is fierce. When dealers are competing for the same customer, price becomes a major factor in the courtship of the customer. Who is to say that an operationally efficient dealer shouldn't be able to sell on a lower margin than its competitors?

The majority of our sales are to commercial clients, like builders, kitchen and bath dealers, and remodelers. We sell to them on lower margin with the expectation of their repeat business. However, with UMRPs on some of our brands, our commercial clients are forced to pay the same price as a retail customer. We walk a fine line: Do we violate UMRP policy to maintain our commercial business, or do we adhere to the policies and get eaten alive by our competition, who may violate the policy?

The irony of this is that the distributors that are enforcing UMRPs are complaining that their sales are off by 20% to 30% for the year. With dealers scared to violate UMRP policies for given brands, some are pushing customers toward nonprice-protected brands. Could this explain why distributor sales are off?

—**Wall Street Journal** (August 28, 2008)

Questions

1. For a class discussion, select either of the above-described markets, research their recent history and current conditions, and then evaluate the current and prospective consequences of producer and consumer surpluses in these markets.
2. The eminent microeconomist Joseph Schumpeter has said that it is a characteristic of free markets ". . . that they are subject to a constant gale of creative destruction." As the managing partner of the well-regarded management consulting firm McKinsey and Company, you have been retained by the Board of the London Stock Exchange to assay the future of the Exchange. The board expects your assessment at their meeting on Monday.

2. Are Markets Always Rational and Efficient?

The behavior of market participants has always been the subject of commentary. Adam Smith noted over two hundred years ago the propensity of market participants to "conspiracy." Lord Keynes, the "father" of macro-economics, described equity market participants as being motivated by "animal spirits." Conversely, Nobel Prize laureate economist Gary Becker has said that consumers and producers in markets can be depended on to act on their "rational expectations." The following article from the editorial page of the *New York Times* describes their view of market efficiencies.

The Behavioral Revolution

Roughly speaking, there are four steps to every decision. First, you perceive a situation. Then you think of possible courses of action. Then you calculate which course is in your best interest. Then you take the action.

Over the past few centuries, public policy analysts have assumed that step three is the most important. Economic models and entire social science disciplines are premised on the assumption that people are mostly engaged in rationally calculating and maximizing their self-interest.

But during this financial crisis, that way of thinking has failed spectacularly. As Alan Greenspan noted in his Congressional testimony last week, he was "shocked" that markets did not work as anticipated. "I made a mistake in presuming that the self-interests of organizations, specifically banks and others, were such as that they were best capable of protecting their own shareholders and their equity in the firms."

So perhaps this will be the moment when we alter our view of decision-making. Perhaps this will be the moment when we shift our focus from step three, rational calculation, to step one, perception.

Perceiving a situation seems, at first glimpse, like a remarkably simple operation. You just look and see what's around. But the operation that seems most simple is actually the most complex, it's just that most of the action takes place below the level of awareness. Looking at and perceiving the world is an active process of meaning-making that shapes and biases the rest of the decision-making chain.

Economists and psychologists have been exploring our perceptual biases for four decades now, with the work of Amos Tversky and Daniel Kahneman, and also with work by people like Richard Thaler, Robert Shiller, John Bargh and Dan Ariely.

My sense is that this financial crisis is going to amount to a coming-out party for behavioral economists and others who are bringing sophisticated psychology to the realm of public policy. At least these folks have plausible explanations for why so many people could have been so gigantically wrong about the risks they were taking.

Nassim Nicholas Taleb has been deeply influenced by this stream of research. Taleb not only has an explanation for what's happening, he saw it coming. His popular books "Fooled by Randomness" and "The Back Swan" were broadsides at the risk-management models used in the financial world and beyond.

In "The Black Swan," Taleb wrote, "The government-sponsored institution Fannie Mae, when I look at its risks, seems to be sitting on a barrel of dynamite, vulnerable to the slightest hiccup." Globalization, he noted, "creates interlocking fragility." He warned that while the growth of giant banks gives the appearance of stability, in reality, it raises the risk of a systemic collapse—"when one fails, they all fail."

Taleb believes that our brains evolved to suit a world much simpler than the one we now face. His writing is idiosyncratic, but he does touch on many of the perceptual biases that distort our thinking: our tendency to see data that confirm our prejudices more vividly than data that contradict them; our tendency to overvalue recent events when anticipating future possibilities; our tendency to spin concurring facts into a single causal narrative; our tendency to applaud our own supposed skill in circumstances when we've actually benefited from dumb luck.

And looking at the financial crisis, it is easy to see dozens of errors of perception. Traders misperceived the possibility of rare events. They got caught in social contagions and reinforced each other's risk assessments. They failed to perceive how tightly linked global networks can transform small events into big disasters.

Taleb is characteristically vituperative about the quantitative risk models, which try to model something that defies modelization. He subscribes to what he calls the tragic vision of humankind, which "believes in the existence of inherent limitations and flaws in the way we think and act and requires an acknowledgement of this fact as a basis for any individual and collective action." If recent events don't underline this worldview, nothing will.

If you start thinking about our faulty perceptions, the first thing you realize is that markets are not perfectly efficient, people are not always good guardians of their own self-interest and there might be limited circumstances when government could usefully slant the decision-making architecture (see "Nudge" by Thaler and Cass Sunstein for proposals). But the second thing you realize is *that government officials are probably going to be even worse perceivers of reality than private business types. Their information feedback mechanism is more limited, and, being deeply politicized, they're even more likely to filter inconvenient facts.*

This meltdown is not just a financial event, but also a cultural one. It's a big, whopping reminder that the human mind is continually trying to perceive things that aren't true, and not perceiving them takes enormous effort.

—David Brooks, *New York Times*
Op-Ed Page (October 28, 2008)

Questions

1. For a class debate, take a position as to the efficiency of free markets to optimally allocate a society's scarce resource. In developing your position give full consideration to the reality that markets reflect the perceptions and decisions of human beings and therefore human behavior.

2. John Maynard Keynes, later Lord Keynes, was elected editor of the *Economic Review* shortly after graduating from Cambridge University. As an economic scholar, professor, and advisor to the British Treasury, he formulated economic theory so that today he is recognized as the "father" of macroeconomics. Yet each morning, working with his brokers over the phone, he made a large fortune "speculating" in the foreign exchange markets while exploiting "animal spirits." On the same point, other economists have argued that it is these very animal spirits that induce entrepreneurs and market participants to innovate, bear risk, and defer consumption in the pursuit of profits. For a class debate, take either the affirmative or negative view of "animal spirits" and advocate for its virtue or infamy.

REVIEW QUESTIONS

1. In a perfectly competitive industry where producing firms do *not* have identical cost curves, which of the following is correct in the long run?
   a. The marginal firm earns positive excess returns while the intramarginal firms earn zero excess returns.
   b. The intramarginal firms earn positive excess returns while the marginal firm earns zero excess returns.
   c. Excess returns of the firm(s) that earn them are comprised entirely of economic rent.
   d. Both **b** and **c** are correct.

2. The imposition of a sales tax leads to a(n)
   a. Reduction of a consumer surplus and an increase of a producer surplus.
   b. Reduction of a producer surplus and an increase of a consumer surplus.
   c. Reduction of both a producer surplus and a consumer surplus.
   d. Increase of both a producer surplus and a consumer surplus.

3. Deadweight loss that results from the imposition of a sales tax can be represented as a
   a. Total reduction of consumer surplus and producer surplus.
   b. Total reduction of consumer surplus and producer surplus less the amount of tax collected by the tax authority.
   c. Total amount of tax collected by the tax authority.
   d. None of the above.

4. Which of the following is TRUE about a monopoly firm?
   a. It always operates in the elastic part of its demand curve.
   b. It produces at a level of output where $P = MC$.
   c. Its supply curve can be represented by the part of its MC curve that lies above its AC curve.
   d. None of the above.

5. Suppose that due to the nature of the product and the technology in industry A, the AC curve for a firm in industry A is downward sloping over a range of output that is large relative to the total market for the product. In this setting, one firm comes to dominate the industry because one (not two or more) firm can produce the total industry output at a lower cost than would be possible if output was produced by two or more firms. This situation is best described as:
   a. Nash monopoly.
   b. Natural monopoly.
   c. Contestable monopoly.
   d. Duopoly.

6. Which of the following is TRUE about the kinked demand curve model?
   a. It applies to monopolistically competitive firms and explains why a firm's administered price does not fluctuate every time that its cost curves shift.
   b. It applies to oligopolies and explains why a firm's administered price does not fluctuate every time that its cost curves shift.
   c. It applies to monopolistically competitive firms and explains why a firm's price increases are matched by its competitors.
   d. It applies to oligopolies and explains why a firm's price increases are matched by its competitors.

7. The preferencing of orders in a competitive dealer market
   a. Makes inventory control more difficult.
   b. Facilitates inventory control.
   c. Is not a common dealer practice.
   d. Both a and c are correct.

8. In 2001, the U.S. stocks changed from trading in $ 0.0625 (one-sixteenth of a dollar) to trading in pennies. In relation to this regulatory change, which of the following statements is correct?
   a. The primary goal of this regulatory initiative was to reduce bid-ask spreads.
   b. Industry switched from fractional pricing to decimal pricing.
   c. The tick size was increased.
   d. Both a and b are correct.

9. What is an inside spread (i.e., a market spread) in a quote-driven market?
   a. The difference between the highest bid of all the dealer firms and the lowest ask of all the dealer firms.
   b. The difference between the highest ask of all of the dealer firms and the lowest bid of all of the dealer firms.
   c. The spread quoted by the primary (largest) market maker in a stock.
   d. None of the above.

10. A network externality
   a. Is illustrated by the air pollution that attends electricity production by a power plant.
   b. Is also referred to as an economy of social behavior.
   c. Is an effect on the entire network (positive or negative) that is produced by an individual's act of joining the network, but one that is not taken into account by this individual.
   d. Can be achieved by excluding the network's least efficient members.

11. A large buyer and a large seller who fail to meet each other in an opening call which is followed by a continuous market illustrates
   a. A Nash equilibrium, because both parties could be better off if they "cooperated," that is, showed up at the opening call.
   b. A Nash equilibrium, because both parties, on expectation, wind up trading at better prices in the continuous market.
   c. Power of Adam Smith's invisible hand that leads both parties to trade at better prices at the continuous market.
   d. How under in a Nash equilibrium individual participants are induced to act irrationally.

12. Which of the following is TRUE about time priority?
   a. It refers to market makers serving their customers in a timely manner.

    b. It refers to rationing excess demand or supply according to a first come, first serve rule.

    c. It characterizes trading in a quote driven dealer market.

    d. All of the above.

13. Which of the following best describes the competition in a competitive dealer market?

    a. Intense price competition that focuses on the size of a bid-ask spread.

    b. Intense nonprice competition to gain a larger percentage of a stock's total order flow.

    c. Mild competition because of the practice of preferencing.

    d. No competition because this market is a monopoly.

14. When a monopolistically competitive firm's marginal cost curve shifts up, in order to maximize profits the firm will

    a. Reduce output and increase price.

    b. Increase output and reduce price.

    c. Increase both output and price.

    d. Reduce both output and price.

15. Which of the following market environments would you expect to yield the greatest product variety?

    a. Monopoly.

    b. Monopolistic competition.

    c. Perfect competition.

    d. Oligopoly.

16. Which of the following is correct?

    a. If there are only two selling firms in a market, prices must be above marginal cost.

    b. If there is only one firm in a market, prices must be above marginal cost.

    c. If there are three selling firms in a market, prices must be above marginal cost.

    d. All of the above.

17. Which of the following is TRUE with regard to a contestable market?

    a. In a contestable market, the industry consists of a sizable number of firms and entry and exit is relatively costless.

    b. In a contestable market, the industry consists of a single firm and it is incented to keep its price relatively low because unduly high profits are likely to attract competitors into the industry.

    c. A defining feature of a contestable market is the availability of close substitutes to its product.

    d. Both a and c are correct.

18. Which of the following is true for perfect competition but not true for monopoly?

    a. $MC = MR.$
    b. $P = MC.$
    c. Increased profits can be realized from employing a price-discriminating strategy.
    d. Both **b** and **c**.
19. Which of the following statements about excess returns, profits, and economic rents in the competitive market is FALSE?
    a. Profits are short-lived and are a part of transition mechanism that brings the industry from one equilibrium to another after a shock occurs.
    b. Profits and economic rents are the two components of the excess returns.
    c. In the long run, excess returns for the firms that realize them consist entirely of economic rents.
    d. Economic rents are short-lived while profits can be sustained by a marginal firm in the long run.
20. A movie theater sells Wednesday show tickets at a lower price than for a weekend show. This is an example of:
    a. Price discrimination.
    b. Predatory pricing.
    c. Collusive pricing.
    d. None of the above.

APPLICATIONS AND ISSUES

Why Do Firms Extend Trade Credit?

As noted in the chapter, competition is intense between firms that face downward sloping demand curves and thus have some power to set their own prices. With regard to monopolistic competition, we wrote that a ". . . firm will strive to differentiate its product better, to advertise, and to have sales promotions, all in an attempt to establish a brand name that distinguishes it from its competition. Product quality and good customer relationships count heavily in this effort." There is something else that the competitive firm will do: extend trade credit to its customers.

Nonfinancial firms commonly extend trade credit to their customers.* A typical set of terms is 2/10 net 30. These terms mean that a firm which is selling a good or a service is telling its buyer, "If you pay within 10 days you

---

*This thought question draws on Robert A. Schwartz, "An Economic Model of Trade Credit," *Journal of Financial and Quantitative Analysis* (September 1974), 643–657.

will get a 2 percent discount and, if not, the entire amount due has to be paid in 30 days." By extending trade credit, the seller is providing financing to the buyer. And so the buyer has obtained two resources, not one, from the seller: the good or service that is being purchased and short-term financial capital. We are accustomed to banks providing short-term financial capital to firms, but they are not the only ones. With trade credit, non-financial firms are also providing short-term funding to each other. Why do they do this?

Two motives can be noted: a finance motive and a transactions motive. The finance motive exists because of the time value of money, because buyers who receive credit from a seller will be better customers. The transaction motive exists because trading is not a frictionless process, because it costs something to match the time pattern of payments with the time pattern of receipts, and trade credit enables the payments to be coordinated more efficiently. The finance and transactions motives both suggest that the demand curve faced by a firm for its product is higher and further to the right when it offers its customers trade credit.

With this by way of background, let's focus on a firm that is facing a downward-sloping demand curve, and consider the relationships between the firm's credit policy, the location of its demand curve, and its product price. Ignore the discount period and concentrate only on the net period (that is, instead of the terms being "2/10, net 30," let them simply be "net 30"). Assume that the seller is a relatively large and established firm, and that its customers are a homogeneous group of smaller, younger firms.

The relevant variables are:

P_L: List price of the product
r_S: Relevant rate of interest for the seller
r_B: Relevant rate of interest for the buyers (assume $r_B > r_S$)
P_S: Present value of the list price received by the seller [$P_S = P_L(1+R_S)^{-T}$]
P_B: Present value of the list price paid by the buyers [$P_B = P_L(1+R_B)^{-T}$]
N: Length of the net period
Q: Quantity of the good sold to the buyer

The questions are:

1. With reference to the *transactions motive*, explain why the selling firm's list price demand curve shifts up and to the right when it extends trade credit to its buyers.
2. With reference to the *finance motive*, how does the rate of interest for the seller and for the buyers depend on the characteristics of these firms

(e.g., their size)? For whom do you expect the rate of interest to be lower, the seller or the buyers? (Remember, we have assumed that the seller, relative to the buyers, is a larger, better established firm.)

3. With reference to the *finance motive*, explain why the selling firm's list price demand curve shifts up and to the right when it extends trade credit to its buyers.

4. Recognizing that the seller can gain knowledge of its buyers through its marketing and sales efforts, how do you think the seller's rate, r_S, compares with a rate that a bank would charge the buyers?

5. Assume $0 < r_S < r_B$ and $N > 0$. What does this imply about the relationship between the list price, the seller's present value price (P_S), and the buyers' present value price (P_B)?

6. Present three demand curves that the seller could use in determining it's credit policy, pricing, and output decisions: (1) a demand curve for $N = 0$, (2) a list price demand curve for $N > 0$, and (3) a present value to the seller of the list price demand curve for $N > 0$.

7. If extending credit to its buyers is profitable for the seller, what economic reality would ensure that N has a finite optimal value?

8. Do you expect that the optimal value of N and the optimal value of Q are positively related or negatively related? Why?

9. Assume that in a period of expanding economic activity and increasingly tight monetary policy, interest rates and credit rationing are increasing, and trade credit is being substituted for bank credit. What might this imply about the efficiency of financial markets and the efficacy of aggregate monetary policy?

Are Monopolies "Natural" or Conspiracies?

The aversion to monopolies is rooted in the autocratic monarchial abuses of the medieval era when royal rulers granted exclusive licenses to favorites and speculators. These royal licenses gave the holder the right to exclusive control of the manufacture and distribution of a good or service such as salt, road passage, cloth, and banking. These abuses of royal authority in many countries led to the ultimate overthrow of monarchies. Modern microeconomic theory views monopoly as a failure of competition and therefore a potential abuse of consumers.

Yet some modern monopolies have arisen out of the creativity of enterprise, economies of scale, and consumer preference. For example, Heinz's ketchup has consistently maintained a 90 percent market share for over 50 years. Exxon-Mobil, I.B.M., and Microsoft have all been the targets of American antimonopoly prosecutions. In these three cases the antimonopoly prosecutions failed, despite evident market domination.

What limits and constraints are appropriate in the prosecution of monopolies as "conspiracies in restraint of trade?"

What Role Is Played by the "Satisfied" Consumer?

Market research suggests that for repetitive consumer products and services obtaining the initial consumer purchase is the most expensive for the seller. The implication is that the second and subsequent consumer purchases of a product or service can be increasingly profitable as the cost of these repeat sales decline for the seller. Therefore assuring consumer/customer satisfaction is fundamental to successful producers. In our discussion of equities market maker operations, the practice of customer preferencing is described. Therein is the concept of "nonprice" competition. What are the components of "nonprice" competition as they evolve into a specific customer preference?

ADDITIONAL READINGS

Clark, Gregory. *A Farewell to Alms.* Princeton, NJ: Princeton University Press, 2007.

An analytic structure of economic development reflecting the forces of demography and knowledge and their mobilization through market pricing.

Mishkin, Frederick. *The Next Great Globalization.* Princeton, NJ: Princeton University Press, 2006.

The evolution of the world's financial markets will provide the optimal means of assuring rising living standards in the third world.

ANSWERS TO REVIEW QUESTIONS

1. d
2. c
3. b
4. a
5. b
6. b
7. a
8. d
9. a
10. c
11. a
12. b
13. b
14. a
15. b
16. d
17. b
18. b
19. d
20. a

CHAPTER 7

Market Efficiency

LEARNING OBJECTIVES

- **Understand the concept of allocation efficiency.** Given that *economics* can be defined as "the study of the optimal allocation of scarce resources among competing needs," you should not be surprised that the efficiency of resource allocation is of fundamental importance. This chapter focuses on the ability of a market to achieve allocation efficiency (goods and services being produced in the right ways and amounts and consumed in the right amounts from a public policy point of view).

- **Comprehend the meaning of the term *market failure*.** It is important to recognize that a micro market can fail to deliver the allocation efficiency that one might desire from a public policy point of view (and that in extreme cases, a micro market may even fail to exist). Chapter 7 enumerates 10 classic causes of market failure.

- **Understand the link between information and expectations.** In an environment characterized by risk and uncertainty, information is the input that participants base their expectations on. Different participants may form identical expectations (referred to as *homogeneous expectations*) or have different expectations (referred to as *divergent expectations*). You should recognize the complexity of information, and be aware that our insights into the workings of a financial market are influenced by whether we assume that participants' expectations are homogeneous, or that they are divergent.

- **Acquire some basic information about information.** A sizable part of this chapter focuses on information that you should see as a driving force for the micro markets. In light of its importance, we consider information a factor of production. The chapter states that "information sets themselves can be enormous, incomplete, imprecise, and inaccurate, and inefficiency in the micro markets can, to no inconsequential extent, be attributed to information-related inefficiencies." An important learning objective is to understand what this entails in greater detail.

■ **Be familiar with the dimensions of informational efficiency.** Various dimensions of informational efficiency should be understood. These include the efficient exploitation of existing information, efficiency with regard to information gathering, the informational accuracy of an equilibrium price, the efficiency of information dissemination, the informational accuracy of a market price, and the efficiency with which prices are actually discovered in the marketplace.

■ **Understand one efficiency test that has been applied to equity markets.** You should become familiar with the Efficient Market Hypothesis (EMH, a centerpiece of modern portfolio theory), and with one important test of the hypothesis—whether stock prices follow random walks. When all information is fully reflected in market prices, future price changes cannot be predicted, prices are fully efficient, and fully efficient prices will follow random walks. Early tests generally confirmed the random walk theory, but an increasing number of more recent tests using high frequency (intraday data) have not. You should understand the importance of the issue and the arguments involved, and sharpen your own thinking about the informational efficiency of financial markets.

■ **Pay particular attention to the efficiency with which appropriate prices for financial securities are discovered in a marketplace.** Price discovery is a major function of a market center, and the speed and efficacy with which asset prices are found is an important measure of a market's efficiency. You should understand that the clarity of price discovery depends on the competitive structure of the industry, on the architecture of a market center, on investor behavior in the market, and on the role that emotions play in securities trading. The line of thinking relating to price discovery opens a door to behavioral economics and, in so doing, raises any number of questions.

■ **Comprehend the "big picture" on financial market efficiency.** While arguments in support of free and competitive markets are powerful, it is preposterous to believe that the free market is always perfectly efficient. On the contrary, there are well-documented causes of market failure, and ten of them are set forth early in the chapter. The chapter also delves into informational inefficiencies. You should form your own opinion about the quality of the link between information and security prices and, accordingly, about the information efficiency of financial markets.

■ **Think about what might be learned from the market turmoil of 2007–2009.** The market turmoil of the recent past illustrates (as do other historical periods) the macroeconomic instability of markets. During this turbulent period, the various sources of market failure were at work, and their joint impact amplified specific market risks into general market turmoil and the specter of extensive systemic risk. The chapter highlights some of the major events in this period and revisits the ten classic causes of market failure identified earlier in the chapter. You should come to your own understanding of (1) why the macro economy spun out of control, and (2) the role played by market failure on the micro markets level.

■ **Consider the greater generality of the frictions problem.** The first paragraph of the last section of the chapter contains the words, " . . . transaction costs exist in all markets, demand and supply conditions in all markets are unstable over time, and all markets require some mechanism for finding the prices at which trades are made. Could it be that the problems facing the equity markets are symptomatic of difficulties that are more pervasive throughout the economy?" The section ends with the words, ". . . one thing is for sure: The market turbulence of 2008 and beyond has given us all a great deal to think about concerning the efficiency of the micro markets." A fundamental learning goal for this chapter is to further structure thinking about the inherent efficiency and also inefficiency of the micro markets.

CHAPTER SUMMARY

Microeconomic theory presents an intriguing and deeply insightful depiction of how households and firms make optimal consumption and production decisions so as to maximize their feelings of well-being (which we call utility) and their profits. Microeconomic theory also takes a second major step: It examines how the individual, self-serving decisions of households and firms interact on the aggregate level. Aggregation is not a simple matter. Until a careful assessment is made, one cannot know if what is good for participants individually is good for everybody collectively. In this chapter, we have not focused per se on the efficiency with which actual households and firms make their decisions, but on the quality of outcomes that the micro markets can deliver for participants in aggregate. Here are the key points that we have made:

1. First the good news. In a plain vanilla, deterministic (nonstochastic), frictionless environment where all participants (firms and

households alike) are atomistic, the equilibrium conditions have excellent properties from a social policy point of view. For all goods, the marginal rate of substitution in consumption is the same for all consumers, the marginal rate of technical substitution in production is the same for all firms, and all prices (which reflect utility on the margin) equal their respective marginal costs of production. With the marginal conditions satisfied, no mutually utility-enhancing (for households) or profit-enhancing (for firms) redistribution of resources between economic agents is possible.

2. Real-world markets, however, are not ideal environments, and they can fail to deliver even close to textbook perfect results. In some extreme cases, a micro market may even fail to operate at all (that is, a market might totally collapse). We consider 10 classic causes of market failure: imperfect and asymmetric information, irrational behavior, short-run myopia, externalities, network externalities, moral hazard, principal-agent problems, public goods attributes, technological inertia, and systemic risk.

3. A daunting challenge facing the micro markets is the complexity, the size, the incompleteness, and the imprecision of much of the information that households and firms base their consumption and production decisions on. With an eye towards the equity markets, we differentiate between *market information* (for instance, quotes, transaction prices, and trading volume) and *fundamental information* (for instance, financial information, management strategy, economic information, structural change, and organizational efficiency). We also subdivide information into *public information* (which is widely disseminated and readily available), *inside information* (possessed by only a select set of insiders), and *private information* (generated by individuals through their own analyses of public information).

4. Participants base their expectations about future outcomes on the information that they currently possess. For a set of participants, expectations can be *homogeneous* (they all form identical expectations) or *divergent* (while having access to the same information, different people do not interpret it the same way and thus come to different conclusions about its meaning). Important formulations (such as the Capital Asset Pricing Model) are based on the assumption that expectations are homogeneous. In real-world markets, however, divergent expectations is the name of the game, and this paradigm shift has major implications (concerning, for instance, how equilibrium prices are discovered in a micro market).

5. Informational efficiency is a multidimensional concept. We consider the efficiency with which investors exploit existing information, the

efficiency with which they pursue information-gathering activities, the informational accuracy of equilibrium prices, and the dynamic efficiency of information dissemination. These are not simple matters. A lot is required for a market to be informationally efficient.

6. As we turn next to a test of market efficiency, we focus on equity markets and on informational efficiency. How does one know, you might wonder, whether all existing information is fully reflected in stock prices? It turns out that there is a very clever way to infer whether prices are being efficiently set. The way involves the *Efficient Market Hypothesis (EMH)*. The hypothesis is that information is fully reflected in stock prices, and the best-known test of the EMH is whether stock prices follow random walks.

7. Here is the logic behind the random-walk tests: If all information is reflected in a stock's price, then there is no way to predict how the stock's price will change in the future, because we would have no way of knowing what the new information will be. But what if future stock price changes are correlated with past stock price changes? With a correlation pattern, future price changes could be predicted from past price changes. But predictability itself is information, and acting on this information eliminates the very correlation patterns that it is based on. Once any correlation message is incorporated in price, the correlation patterns can no longer exist and price must be following a random walk.

8. Earlier tests broadly supported the random-walk hypothesis. But with the advent of high frequency (intraday) data and new econometric techniques, evidence is accumulating that correlation patterns do exist in stock returns. The random-walk hypothesis is not as stellar today as it once was.

9. Having established that correlation patterns do exist in stock returns data, we introduced a fifth informational efficiency criterion: the efficiency with which prices are discovered in the marketplace. Having previously presented 10 classic causes of market failure, we added noisy price discovery as an eleventh cause.

   Price discovery is not fully efficient to the extent that it works its way out over time while trades are being made. The market is always searching for a sustainable equilibrium value but does not necessarily find one before a demand shift changes the equilibrium value that the market has been trying to discover.

10. We clarified that the efficiency of price discovery depends in part on the structure of the marketplace where the trades are being made. The complexity of price discovery also reflects the fact that investors are less than textbook efficient information processing machines.

11. Our price discovery story has three parts that moved from fuzzy assessments, to divergent expectations, to adaptive valuations. And it has three punch lines: (1) A market is a network within which no one participant alone establishes an equilibrium price. (2) A stock does not have a *unique* equilibrium price; its price, which is discovered in the marketplace, depends on how the separate evaluations of the various participants are communicated between the members of the group. (3) The equilibrium value that is discovered for a stock is path dependent. Namely, after any shift in investor desires to hold shares of a stock, the path followed during the early stages of the adjustment process affects the value that the path will eventually converge on.

12. Recognizing price discovery as a dynamic process accomplishes several things. It opens the door to behavioral economics, it provides a raison d'être for technical analysis and algorithmic trading, and it offers an explanation of why intraday prices are as volatile as we observe them to be, especially at the opening of a trading session and then again at the close.

13. The big picture that we have presented on financial market efficiency is that markets may well be less than perfectly efficient. For many practitioners, this will not appear to be a revelation. But microeconomists have long seen and respected the inherent efficiency of free and competitive markets, and financial economists have found additional validation in their empirical studies of stock price movements. We respect these findings. The point is, the equity markets are not 100 percent efficient. Should we look at the percent of the glass that is full whatever that percentage might be (e.g., 90 percent), or at the percent that is empty (e.g., 10 percent). We call attention to "the 10 percent," and we stress the importance of seeing it as such. Our quotes from Graham and Dodd, from Lawrence Summers, and from Bernard Baruch are in keeping with this thinking.

14. The financial turmoil that had its roots in 2007 of 2008 and that hit markets around the world in 2008, underscored the problems that can beset the micro markets. We turned to the recent (and ongoing) events in the next section of the chapter. In so doing, we first paid attention to four concepts: risk, uncertainty (which is differentiated from risk), volatility that can characterize free and competitive markets, and systemic risk. We then revisited the 10 causes of market failure to get a taste of the role that each of them played in the debacle of 2008.

15. The final topic in this chapter was the greater generality of the frictions problem. We have focused on one market: the equity market. But to better understand one market is to open one's eyes to realities that may exist far more broadly in the micro markets. Friction (including

imperfect information) clearly impacts the workings of the equity markets. How about other markets? The equity markets move with lightning speed—as of 9:30 in the morning, 12:00 noon might be the long run. Housing markets, many labor markets, and most other markets move at a far slower pace. Nevertheless, they all face the frictions problem. Is price discovery unique to the equity markets? The very writing of a contract, once it has been signed, imposes a large adjustment cost or, in our terminology, a friction. How are prices determined while a contract is being written? Matters such as the negotiation of an administered price aside, price discovery is certainly an issue in, say, the writing of a three-year labor contract. We underscore the importance of understanding the issue.

16. We ended the chapter with the thought that it is not a matter of free markets versus regulated markets, or of deregulation versus reregulation. Appropriate regulation is certainly needed. But how do we get it? What is the proper balance between the discipline inherent in a free market and the rules, regulations, and enforcements imposed by government? In this chapter, we focused on the abilities of free markets to deliver desired results, but we have also devoted much attention to the inefficiencies of a free market. Does this call for government to step up and play a more decisive role? In the next chapter we turn to issues concerning government regulation.

GLOSSARY

adaptive valuations As applied to equity trading, the phenomenon of an investor changing from a bearish valuation to a bullish valuation, or vice versa, upon learning the valuations of others. A seller becoming a buyer, or vice versa.

algorithmic trading Computer-driven trading. Algos are computer resident trading rules that electronically generate buy and sell orders.

allocational efficiency Producing and consuming goods and services in optimal proportions. For instance, a consumer is optimally allocated income between two goods (call them X and Y) when the ratio of marginal utilities for the two goods equals the ratio of their market prices. Similarly, is efficiently using two inputs into production (call them labor and capital) when the ratio of their marginal products equals the ratio of their market prices.

asymmetric information Some market participants are in possession of some information that other participants do not have.

behavioral economics Analysis of economic decisions that are made by agents, not entirely according to rational economic principles, but also in light of cognitive and emotional factors, and bounded rationality.

contract curve   A line showing the efficient allocations of two resources between two participant. The locus of all points of tangency between the indifference curves of the two participants when the indifference curves of one of them has been rotated 180 degrees. *See also* Edgeworth box.

divergent expectations   Different investors in possession of the same information have different risk and return expectations for a security. Heterogeneous as distinct from homogeneous expectations.

economic information   Information concerning the firm's product market, the firm's competitors, national and international economic conditions, and so on.

Edgeworth box   A diagram showing all possible allocations of given amounts of two inputs between two consumers. *See also* contract curve.

efficient market hypothesis (EMH)   The hypothesis that all existing information is fully reflected in share values. No trader can trade profitably (realize above normal, risk-adjusted returns) based on already existing information.

financial information   Information concerning a firm's current capital structure, earnings forecasts, and so on.

fundamental information   Economic and financial information pertaining to the determinants of future share values. Fundamental as distinct from market information.

high-frequency data   Intraday trade and quotations data. The complete record of all trades and quotes.

homogeneous expectations   Investors in possession of the same information have the same risk and return expectations for a security. Homogeneous as distinct from divergent (i.e., heterogeneous) expectations.

informational efficiency   The accuracy with which prices that are set in a marketplace reflect the underlying information that participant expectations are based on.

inside information   Information possessed by a select set of people who have a special access to information. Corporate officers and others with business ties to a company (such as an investment banker, lawyer, or proofreader) are commonly in possession of "inside information." Trading based on inside information is illegal.

interdependent valuations   Investor reassessments of their individual valuations that are based on what they know about others' valuations. *See also* adaptive valuations.

management strategy   Knowledge of the strategic business decisions of management that is based on management's assessment of current conditions, and on its outlook for the future.

market breakdown (failure)   When a specific market fails to achieve an efficient market outcome from a public policy point of view. The failure can be in terms of price established and/or quantity traded. It can be attributable to factors such as externalities, asymmetric information, or moral hazard problems. In the extreme, a market can actually shut down (that is, totally ceases operations).

market information   Information about current market conditions including current market quotes, transaction prices, and transaction volumes.

moral hazard   A situation that exists when a decision maker who does not bear the full responsibility for all possible outcomes acts more recklessly than he or she otherwise would and thereby imposes a cost on others.

negative externalities   An action involving the production, exchange, or consumption of a good or service that imposes a cost on others who are not directly involved in the action.

network externality   When the users of a product can be viewed as having formed a network, and where the value of the network for the users increases with the number of members in the network. No one participant, in deciding whether or not to join a network, takes into account the value that his or her joining would have for others, which accounts for the use of the term *externality*. Fax machines are a good example of a network (the more people who have a fax machine, the more people anyone with such a machine can send a fax to), but nobody while buying a fax machine takes account of the benefit that his/her purchase will bestow on others.

path dependent   The final, sustainable value a variable (such as price) converges on depends on the specific path that the variable has followed during the earlier part of its value discovery process.

positive externalities   An action involving the production, exchange, or consumption of a good or service that benefits others who are not directly involved in the action. Some externalities can be internal to an industry but external to the individual firms in the industry; such economies lower the average cost curves for the individual firms as the industry expands (for instance, a larger industry may, through a central organization, be able to provide better information at lower cost to the individual firms that are its members).

price discovery   In any micro market, price discovery is the process of finding an equilibrium value for a good, service, or productive resource that is being traded. Price discovery is a complex, imperfect process when participants do not simultaneously reveal their complete demand and supply functions. In an equity market, price discovery is the dynamic process of finding a value that best reflects the broad market's desire to hold shares of a stock. In equity markets, price discovery occurs most prominently after the receipt of news and following market openings as prices adjust to new economic conditions and to changes in the investors' desires to hold shares.

principal-agent problem   A problem that arises when, due to incomplete contracting, an agent's own interests are in conflict with those of the principal who has hired him.

private information   Information about a stock that individuals possess because of their own investigations and analyses.

public goods   Goods that nonusers cannot be excluded from consuming. Goods for which one person's consumption does not reduce the availability of the good for others. A lighthouse in the harbor is a classic example of a public good; all ships passing can pick up the signal and one ship picking up the signal does not lessen the signal that other ships can receive.

public information   Widely disseminated information that all public participants can obtain.

quants   Market participants using advanced mathematical techniques to value assets, formulate investment strategies, make trading decisions, and so on.

random walk   When the next step that an individual takes is totally independent of all of the steps that he/she has been previously taken, the person is said to be taking a "random walk." The term is used with regard to the dynamic behavior of stock prices when the next return for a stock (the stock's next "step") is not correlated with the stock's past returns (previous "steps"), and the next price change for a stock is totally unpredictable.

Reg. FD   The SEC's 2000 rule that any listed company must immediately publicly disclose any information once the information has been provided to any public participant.

stochastic values   Values that are not deterministic. Nonrandom values.

systemic risk   *See* Nondiversifiable risk.

technical analysis (charting)   The use of recent price data to predict future price movements.

CURRENT EVENTS DISCUSSIONS

1. When and by Whom Should Markets Be "Regulated"?

Our focus on the securities markets has given us an opportunity to review market efficiency and inefficiency in the financial market turmoil that evolved from the summer of 2007 through the summer of 2009. While our financial markets received most of the media attention, we should not forget the volatility of other markets for such things as commodities, which saw crude oils spike to $147 a barrel in August 2008, only to collapse to $39 a barrel four months later. Winter wheat, which was at $19 a bushel in the spring of 2008 was at $5 a bushel by year end. The informational efficiencies of these markets were clearly tested in the extreme during this market turmoil. Yet it is the financial markets that were the greatest sources of emotion and hazard as the turmoil unfolded.

In response, the London *Economist* cautioned early in the turmoil that rash "regulation" of markets would be destructive. The following articles are two detailed discussions of the overall issue of market regulation, and the specific contribution to the market upheaval by principal market participants. The *New York Times* and the *Wall Street Journal* have also expressed views concerning the events that comprise the financial markets turmoil. These articles should be evaluated together. Thereafter, the student can consider and respond to the two assignments at the end.

Credit Crisis: Fixing Finance

Crises are endemic to financial systems. Attempts to regulate them may do more harm than good.

As if collapsing prices were not enough, American mortgage firms now have to cope with home rage. Borrowers vent their fury on the system that is repossessing their properties by smashing holes in walls and tipping paint over living-room carpets. Something similar is going on in the house finance built. Faith in open markets has been poisoned by a crisis that has spread from one asset to the next. First there was disbelief and denial. Then fear. Now comes anger.

For three decades, public policy has been dominated by the power of markets—flexible and resilient, harnessing self-interest for the public good, and better than any planner-in-chief. Nowhere are markets deeper and more liquid than in modern finance. But finance has stumbled and there are growing calls from all sides for bold reregulation.

New rules became inevitable the moment the Federal Reserve rescued Bear Stearns and pledged to lend to other Wall Street banks. If taxpayers are required to bail out investment banks, the governments need to impose tighter limits on the risks those banks can take. This week Hank Paulson, America's treasury secretary, unveiled a longer-term plan to deal with this and other weaknesses in America's regulatory system; and next week the G7 finance ministers will meet in Washington, DC, where they will discuss a report on the crisis by the Financial Stability Forum.

It is natural and right that regulators should seek to learn lessons. The credit crisis will damage not just the reputation of the financial system but also the lives of those who lose their houses, businesses and jobs as a result of it. But before governments set about reforming financial regulation, they need both to be clear about the causes of the crisis and to understand just how little regulators can achieve.

Arm's-Length Finance

The history of financial markets is not a stable one. They have imploded every decade or so, whether because French and Spanish kings reneged on their debt in the 16th century or because speculators inflated railway stock in the 19th century. But this crisis is unusually shocking, if only because the mild business cycle and the fast pace of world economic growth in recent years had lulled people into a false sense of security.

The view that the only sensible response to the 21st century's first serious financial crisis is a wholesale reform of the system is now gaining ground. Josef Ackermann, über-capitalist and chief executive of Deutsche Bank, summed it up in a call for governments to step in: "I no longer believe in the market's self-healing power." The implication is that, if the market cannot heal the wounds it sustains as a result of its own risky behaviour, then it must be discouraged from taking such risks in the first place.

But there are two reasons to hesitate before plunging headlong into a purge of the system. First, finance was not solely to blame for the crisis. Lax monetary policy also played a starring role. Low interest rates boosted the prices of assets, especially of housing, which in turn fed into complex debt securities. This created a spiral of debt that is only now being unwound. True, monetary policy is too blunt a tool to manage asset prices with, but, as the IMF now says, central banks in economies with deep mortgage markets should in future lean against the wind when house prices are rising fast.

The second reason to hesitate is that bold reregulation could damage the very economies it is designed to protect. At times like this, the temptation is for tighter controls to rein in risk-takers, so that those regular, painful crashes could be avoided. It is an honourable aim, but a mistaken one.

The Inevitable Crash

Finance is a brain for matching labour to capital, for allowing savers and borrowers to defer consumption or bring it forward, for enabling people to share, and trade, risks. The smarter the system is, the better it will do that. A poorly functioning system will back wasteful schemes and shun worthy ones, trap people in the present, heap risk on them and slow economic growth. This puts finance in a dilemma. A sophisticated and innovative financial system is susceptible to destructive booms; but a simple, tightly regulated one will condemn an economy to grow slowly.

The tempting answer is to try to wriggle free from the dilemma with a compromise that would permit innovation but exert just enough control to squeeze out financial failure. It is a nice idea; but it is a fantasy. The experience of the past year is an object lesson in the limited power of regulators.

Just look at their mistakes. Before the crisis, hedge funds were regarded with suspicion as vulnerable and irresponsible. But, with a few notable exceptions, they have weathered the storm less as *culprits than as victims. Instead, the system's own safety features turned out to be its weakest points. The copper bottom fell out of AAA bonds when housing markets failed to do what the rating agencies had expected. Banks avoided rules requiring them to put aside capital, by warehousing vast sums off-balance sheet with disastrous results.*

It would be convenient to blame the regulators for all that, but the system is stacked against them. They are paid less than those they oversee. They know less, they may be less able, they think like the financial herd, and they are shackled by politics. In an open economy, business can escape a regulatory squeeze in one country by skipping offshore. Once a bubble is inflating many factors conspire to discourage a regulator from pricking it.

And even if you could put all that right, regulators would still fail, because of the nature of finance itself. Financial progress is about learning to deal with strangers in more complex ways. The village moneylender, limited by his need to know those he did business with, was gradually superseded by ever-broader impersonal markets that can cheaply mobilise colossal sums and sell more complex products. The remarkable thing is not that finance suffers from booms and busts, but that it works at all. People who would not dream of lending £1,000 to that nice family three doors down routinely hand over their life savings to strangers in a South Korean chaebol or an Atlantan start-up. It all depends on trust.

Regulators cannot know how trust will ebb and flow as new markets develop the experience and practice they need to work better. They therefore cannot predict the peril of new ideas. They have to let new markets develop, or stifle them. The system learns—dangerous junk bonds are reborn as respectable high-yield debt; bankers will now be scared of extreme leverage—but it is delicate, as the world learned last summer. The regulator is condemned to muddle through.

The notion that the world can just regulate its way out of crises is thus an illusion. Rather, crisis is the price of innovation, so governments face a choice. They can embrace new financial ideas by keeping markets open. Regulation will be light, but there will be busts. The state will sometimes have to clear up and regulation must be about cure as well as prevention. Or governments can aim for safety and opt for dumbed-down financial systems that hobble their economies and deprive their people of the benefits of faster growth. And even then a crisis may strike.

—***The Economist*** (April 3, 2008)

2. Does Government Contribute to Market Volatility?

At the center of the financial turmoil that emerged in the summer and fall of 2008 was the home mortgage lending activities of several government agencies, including the Federal National Mortgage Association (Fannie Mae), the Federal Home Loan Mortgage Acceptance Corporation (Freddie Mac), the Department of Housing and Community Renewal, the Federal Housing Administration, the Treasury Department, and others. The appearance to investors of government "backing" of the home mortgages and their derivative "mortgage-backed securities" created a moral hazard. In addition, political leaders saw home ownership as a "public good." Compounding this informational inefficiency was a principal-agent tension among the officers of these government sponsored entities. The below abridgement from the *New York Times* describes the contribution of one of these government-sponsored entities to the market failure of 2007–2009.

Pressured to Take More Risk, Fannie Reached Tipping Point

"Almost no one expected what was coming. It's not fair to blame us for not predicting the unthinkable."— Daniel H. Mudd, *former chief executive, Fannie Mae.*

But by the time Mr. Mudd became Fannie's chief executive in 2004, his company was under siege. Competitors were snatching lucrative parts of its business. Congress was demanding that Mr. Mudd help steer more loans to low-income borrowers. Lenders were threatening to sell directly to Wall Street unless Fannie bought a bigger chunk of their riskiest loans.

So Mr. Mudd made a fateful choice. Disregarding warnings from his managers that lenders were making too many loans that would never be repaid, he steered Fannie into more treacherous corners of the mortgage market, according to executives.

For a time, that decision proved profitable. In the end, it nearly destroyed the company and threatened to drag down the housing market and the economy.

Mr. Mudd said in an interview that he responded as best he could given the company's challenges, and worked to balance risks prudently. "Fannie Mae faced the danger that the market would pass us by," he said. "We were afraid that lenders would be selling products we weren't buying and Congress would feel like we weren't fulfilling our mission. The market was changing, and it's our job to buy loans, so we had to change as well."

Fannie never actually made loans. It was essentially a mortgage insurance company, buying mortgages, keeping some but reselling most to investors and, for a fee, promising to pay off a loan if the borrower defaulted. The only real danger was that the company might guarantee questionable mortgages and lose out when large numbers of borrowers walked away from their obligations.

So Fannie constructed a vast network of computer programs and mathematical formulas that analyzed its millions of daily transactions and ranked borrowers according to their risk. Those computer programs seemingly turned Fannie into a divining rod, capable of separating pools of similar-seeming borrowers into safe and risky bets. The riskier the loan, the more Fannie charged to handle it. In theory, those high fees would offset any losses.

The ripple effect of Fannie's plunge into riskier lending was profound. Fannie's stamp of approval made shunned borrowers and complex loans more acceptable to other lenders, particularly small and less sophisticated banks. Within a few years of Mr. Mudd's arrival, Fannie was the most powerful mortgage company on earth.

Then it began to crumble.

Regulators, spurred by the revelation of a wide-ranging accounting fraud at Freddie, began scrutinizing Fannie's books. In 2004 they accused Fannie of fraudulently concealing expenses to make its profits look bigger. Mr. Mudd was quickly promoted to the top spot. But the company he inherited was becoming a shadow of its former self.

Shortly after he became chief executive, Mr. Mudd traveled to the California offices of Angelo R. Mozilo, the head of Countrywide Financial, then the nation's largest mortgage lender. Fannie had a longstanding and lucrative relationship with Countrywide, which sold more loans to Fannie than anyone else.

"You're becoming irrelevant," Mr. Mozilo told Mr. Mudd, "You need us more than we need you and if you don't take these loans, you'll find you can lose much more." Investors were also pressuring Mr. Mudd to take greater risks.

Capitol Hill bore down on Mr. Mudd as well. The same year he took the top position, regulators sharply increased Fannie's affordable-housing goals. Democratic lawmakers demanded that the company buy more loans that had been made to low-income and minority homebuyers. But Fannie's computer systems could not fully analyze many of the risky loans that customers, investors and lawmakers wanted Mr. Mudd to buy. Many of them—like balloon-rate mortgages or mortgages that did not require paper-work—were so new that dangerous bets could not be identified. Even so, Fannie began buying huge numbers of riskier loans.

Between 2005 and 2007, the company's acquisitions of mortgages with down payments of less than 10 percent almost tripled. As the market for risky loans soared to $1 trillion, Fannie expanded in white-hot real estate areas like California and Florida.

For two years, Mr. Mudd operated without a permanent chief risk officer to guard against unhealthy hazards. When Enrico Dallavecchia was hired for that position in 2006, he told Mr. Mudd that the company should be charging more to handle risky loans. Mr. Dallavecchia was among those whom Mr. Mudd forced out of the company during a reorganization in August.

But, of course, the moment of truth did arrive. In the middle of last year it became clear that millions of borrowers would stop paying their mortgages. For Fannie, this raised the terrifying prospect of paying billions of dollars to honor its guarantees. Lawmakers, particularly Democrats, leaned on Fannie and Freddie to buy and hold those troubled debts, hoping that removing them from the system would help the economy recover. The companies, eager to regain market share and buy what they thought were undervalued loans, rushed to comply.

"I'm not worried about Fannie and Freddie's health, I'm worried that they won't do enough to help out the economy," the chairman of the House Financial Services Committee, Barney Frank, Democrat of Massachusetts, said at the time. "That's why I've supported them all these years—so that they can help at a time like this."

As the housing crisis worsened, Fannie and Freddie announced larger losses, and their shares prices continued falling.

In July, Secretary of the Treasury Paulson asked Congress for authority to take over Fannie and Freddie, though he said he hoped never to use it. "If you've got a bazooka and people know you've got it, you may not have to take it out," he told Congress.

Mr. Mudd called Treasury weekly. He offered to resign, to replace his board, to sell stock, and to raise debt. "We'll sign in blood anything you want," he told Treasury officials. Mr. Mudd told Treasury that those options would work only if government officials publicly clarified whether they intended to take over Fannie. Otherwise, potential investors would refuse to buy the stock for fear of being wiped out.

Then, last month, Mr. Mudd was instructed to report to the Treasury. Mr. Paulson told Mr. Mudd that he could either agree to a takeover or have one forced upon him. "This is the right thing to do for the economy," Mr. Paulson said, according to two people with knowledge of the talks. "We can't take any more risks." Freddie was given the same message. Less than 48 hours later, Mr. Lockhart and Mr. Paulson ended Fannie and Freddie's independence, with up to $200 billion in taxpayer money to replenish the companies' coffers.

Today, Mr. Paulson is scrambling to carry out a $700 billion plan to bail out the financial sector, while the Treasury effectively runs Fannie and Freddie.

But Mr. Mudd, who lost millions of dollars as the company's stock declined and had his severance revoked after the company was seized, often travels to New York for job interviews. He recalled that one of his sons recently asked him why he had been fired.

"Sometimes things don't work out, no matter how hard you try," he replied.

—Charles Duhigg, *New York Times*
(October 5, 2008; abridged version of article)

3. Do Markets Have the Capacity to Correct Themselves?

As the tumult in the financial markets evolved between the summer of 2007 and the summer of 2009 much of the commentary in the media focused on the apparent complexity of the securities and derivatives traded in those markets. The below article from the *Wall Street Journal* views one segment of those markets and notes that it has not responded with the irrationality that seemed to affect other financial segments.

C.D.S. Market Works Well

The Meltdown That Wasn't
A Primer on Credit Default Swaps, the Latest Beltway Scapegoat

On Friday, the Federal Reserve, SEC and CFTC announced an agreement to begin anointing "central counterparties" for the credit default swap [CDS] market. Before the pols create still more institutions that are too big to fail, and further endanger taxpayers, they might want to spend time defining the problem they intend to solve.

The same goes for House Oversight Chairman Henry Waxman. On Thursday he held his latest hearing designed to blame everything other than failed housing policy for the credit debacle. Eager to avoid being scapegoated, hedge-fund managers at the hearing agreed that the credit default swap market is a problem in need of a regulatory solution. But no matter how many financiers can be made to swear under the hot lights that credit default swaps are the problem, reality is not cooperating with this politically convenient theory. This derivatives market continues to perform better than the market from which it is derived.

Mr. Waxman's committee exists to stage show trials; he doesn't have jurisdiction to legislate about credit markets or anything else. But his media events are helpful to his comrade in exculpation, Barney Frank. The House Financial Services Chairman is among the most desperate to blame something other than housing, where he famously vowed to "roll the dice" with Fannie Mae. He too has fingered credit default swaps and now promises "sensible" regulation. If he does to this market what he did to housing, he will again be rolling the dice with other people's money.

Credit default swaps are contracts that insure against a borrower defaulting on its bonds. The buyer of a CDS contract essentially pays annual premiums and the seller agrees to pay back the principal if the issuer of the bonds doesn't. It's different from insurance in that an investor doesn't actually have to own the underlying bonds—he can simply buy a CDS as a way to make a bearish bet on a company or to offset other risks.

Shattering Beltway illusions, the unregulated CDS market is holding up better than the regulated bond market. Here we are more than a year into the credit meltdown and the CDS market is offering more liquidity than the actual cash market. Eraj Shirvani at Credit Suisse notes that "over the last 18 months, the CDS market—not the bond market—has been the only functioning market that has consistently allowed market participants to hedge or express a credit view."

Large investors have often struggled mightily this autumn to find buyers for their bonds, but they could still trade CDS. The U.K. government seems to agree this is a good thing. Her Majesty's Treasury has recognized the CDS market as an efficient mechanism for setting prices by using it as the benchmark to set the rates in its Credit Guarantee Scheme for banks.

In the U.S., meanwhile, the market has spoken, and CDS contracts are the way that investors now price credit. This means Congress should tread very carefully unless it wants to prolong the *downturn. In an environment in which fewer companies are able to issue bonds and trading is light, a liquid CDS market that can put a price on credit will hasten the day when more companies are able to borrow money to build their businesses. A Congressional over-reaction or too heavy a hand from the New York Fed could delay needed capital from reaching Main Street.*

But the Beltway crowd has a vague sense that while they may not understand this market, financial Armageddon will result when a major participant fails. Lehman Brothers was supposed to be exhibit A. The firm was on one end of roughly $5 trillion in CDS contracts, according to Moody's, and Lehman was itself the subject of $72 billion in CDS, in which other investors were betting on Lehman's success or failure. Here was the doomsday scenario, with a major player in CDS going bankrupt.

It turned out to be the meltdown that never melted. Amazing as it is to Washington ears, those greedy, crazy people running large financial institutions did a decent job of managing their exposures to Lehman. When large banks and insurance companies were vulnerable to Lehman, many had offsetting trades that paid off when Lehman went bust. The net amount of $6 billion owed by sellers of credit protection on Lehman was far smaller than expected and was arrived at through the same orderly settlement auction process that has smoothly managed about a dozen such failures—and all without government regulation.

This is not to say that Lehman's failure didn't damage credit markets. But the problem was not a failure of the CDS market, nor was Lehman's failure caused by CDS. Toxic mortgages killed Lehman. Once Lehman went bust, CDS contracts added relatively little stress to other banks. The stress came from the failure of a big investment bank, which made people unwilling to lend to other banks.

Identifying major systemic risks in the CDS market has proven much harder than the pols expected. The big dealers that trade CDS often demand collateral from customers who owe them money on a trade. But these big dealers usually don't post collateral when the roles are reversed and they owe the customer. While this is not necessarily a sweet deal for small hedge funds doing business with a Goldman or a J.P. Morgan, it minimizes counterparty risks for the major firms. Also, the large dealers generally make their money facilitating trades for customers, not betting one way or another on corporate defaults. So if they sell a lot of credit protection to one customer, they will seek to buy it from somebody else.

AIG, by contrast, was almost entirely a seller of CDS. By sell-ing credit protection on mortgage-backed securities, the firm used CDS to make a big bet on housing, which again is the cause of this crisis. Meanwhile, the search continues for the major counterparty that would have been destroyed by AIG's collapse. As for Mr. Waxman, he should spend more time investigating the cause, not the effects, of market turmoil. Mr. Frank would seem to be the per-fect witness.

—Wall Street Journal (November 15, 2008)

Questions

1. It is often said that free markets are adversarial arenas where buyers compete with one another, sellers compete with each other, and buyers compete with sellers. While in microeconomic theory this competition leads to the optimal allocation of scarce resources, the market process is fraught with the conflicts engendered by the inherent competitive na-ture of markets. Information becomes the crucial determinant for suc-cess among buyers and sellers. In the above discussions of the roots of the financial crisis of 2007–2009, the question of what decision makers knew and when they knew it is the "root" issue. For a class discussion of the financial crisis, evaluate and be prepared to defend your interpre-tation of the conduct of one of the major decision makers described in the above discussions.
2. Just as there are issues of "moral hazard," divergent expectations, and market failure among participants in free markets, similar behavioral issues exist among borrowers and lenders in the credit and money mar-kets. Management of firms can be seen as the "agents" of the share-holder "principals." Therefore, while informational efficiency is a public good, such efficiency does not always prevail. As a newly appointed referee of the 2nd District Federal Court in New York you have been assigned by the presiding judge the task of evaluating the presence of "moral hazard" in the policies, management strategy, and executives of the Federal National Mortgage Association in the period 2004 to 2008. Your report is due on Friday.

REVIEW QUESTIONS

1. In an Edgeworth box diagram, which of the following is TRUE about the move from a point that is not on the contract curve to some point that lies anywhere along the contract curve?

   a. Such a move must be utility enhancing for both individuals.
   b. Such a move cannot possibly be utility enhancing for both individuals.
   c. Such a move will be utility enhancing for at least one individual.
   d. None of the above.
2. Which of the following is NOT among the 10 classic conditions under which market can fail?
   a. Systemic risk.
   b. Distributional inertia.
   c. Short-run myopia.
   d. Principal-agent problems.
3. Which of the following is NOT fundamental information about a Company A stock?
   a. Most recent financial statements of Company A.
   b. Latest transaction prices for Company A stock.
   c. News about an upcoming divesture of a Company A's business unit.
   d. News about a new bond issue by Company A.
4. Which of the following is TRUE about homogeneous expectations?
   a. In the context of equity markets and portfolio management, the homogeneity of expectations is a natural property of investor rationality.
   b. Homogeneous expectations imply that people in possession of the same fundamental information will produce private information.
   c. Homogeneous expectations are highly descriptive of the reality and for that reason are frequently used in theoretical modeling.
   d. Homogeneous expectations imply that if two people are given the same information about the stock, they will come to the same conclusion about the stock value.
5. A partial market failure is best described as a situation where
   a. Government imposes a sales tax.
   b. Short-run demand and supply responses are less elastic than the long-run responses.
   c. Free market fails to satisfy fully the optimality conditions for allocation efficiency in consumption and production.
   d. Market participants have difficulty finding each other without an intervention of an intermediary.
6. Short-run myopia refers to
   a. The asymmetry of information.
   b. Applying an unjustifiably high discount rate to future events.
   c. Ignoring the positive externalities associated with a firm's production process.
   d. Technological inertia.

7. Informational efficiency has which of the following dimensions?
   a. Utilization of the existing information set.
   b. The extent and intensity of information gathering activities.
   c. The dynamic process of information dissemination.
   d. All of the above.

8. Having adaptive valuations implies that investors' expectations concerning future share values may change
   a. If new information becomes available.
   b. When their cash flow needs change.
   c. Upon learning the valuations of others.
   d. When their wealth changes.

9. A stock's price follows a random walk if
   a. Past price movements do not contain any useful information for predicting future price movements.
   b. Stock price changes have no relationship to changes in the relevant information set.
   c. Stock returns contain some correlation patterns.
   d. All of the above is correct.

10. Algorithmic trading refers to the
    a. Analysis of the past price behavior to predict future price movements.
    b. Computer-driven trading rules that formulate trading decisions based on observed stock price behavior and send out orders to trade.
    c. Utilization of random-walk properties of stock prices to formulate profitable trading strategies.
    d. None of the above.

11. If no excess investment returns can be realized from trading on the basis of any information that is publicly available (including past prices), the market is
    a. Strong form efficient.
    b. Semi-strong form efficient.
    c. Weak form efficient.
    d. Mild form efficient.

12. Which of the following is FALSE in the framework of divergent expectations and adaptive valuations?
    a. Stock prices do not have unique fundamental values.
    b. Stock prices are "discovered" as buyers and sellers interact in the marketplace and buy and sell orders are submitted to the marketplace and turned into trades.
    c. Adaptive valuations reflect the homogeneity of market participants.
    d. The equilibrium stock price that is discovered in the marketplace is not a unique value, as the price that the market converges on depends on the path that the search process has taken.

13. Which of the following statements characterizes a public good?
    a. One individual's consumption of the good does not reduce the amount that is available for others to consume.
    b. Users are not individually charged for consuming a public good because it is not possible to preclude nonpayers from consuming it.
    c. Public goods are free for the society in aggregate.
    d. Both **a** and **b** are correct.
14. Which of the following statements about information is FALSE?
    a. Information sets are easily translated into unique fundamental share values that all informed investors will agree on.
    b. Information plays an important role in the economy.
    c. Extreme informational asymmetry can cause a market to collapse.
    d. It is always desirable to be better informed than the party with whom you are trading.
15. A rock star being less careful of her jewelry because it is heavily insured is an example of
    a. Divergent expectations.
    b. Moral hazard.
    c. Risk aversion.
    d. Risk tolerance.

APPLICATIONS AND ISSUES

Does the History of Market Regulation Reveal Patterns of Success?

In our discussion of market efficiencies and inefficiencies, we have focused on the tumultuous financial markets turmoil of the fall of 2007 through the summer of 2009. In part the volatile price movements in the markets for commodities, financial securities, and real estate, as well as the declines of indicators of economic activity, are related to the normal "business cycle." Conversely, some economists have seen "market failures" related to moral hazard, principal-agent problems, systemic risks, and irrational behavior. While our discussion of the equities markets is illustrative of microeconomic principles, turmoil and volatility have prevailed in other markets, such as these for the factors of production. In the following and concluding chapter, we will address the response of the government to these spasms of turmoil and volatility. Yet we should take this opportunity to consider market efficiencies and inefficiencies as they have recently occurred in the broader realm of the factors of production: land, labor, capital, technology, and management skill. These considerations should include an historical perspective of past periods of market turmoil and volatility.

For a set of class discussions, teams can be formed to research, evaluate, appraise, and recommend corrective actions for the different markets for the factors of production. Discussions can include the real estate markets, the labor markets, the commodities markets (specific commodities such as crude oil, grains, metals, and fibers can be considered), and of course the financial markets (including such sectors as the money market, the debt market, the equities market, the derivatives market, and the market for private equity).

Does Product and Market Innovation Confound Regulation?

Here is a schematic of the collateralized debt obligation process. This process is alleged to be the root cause of our recent financial markets turmoil.

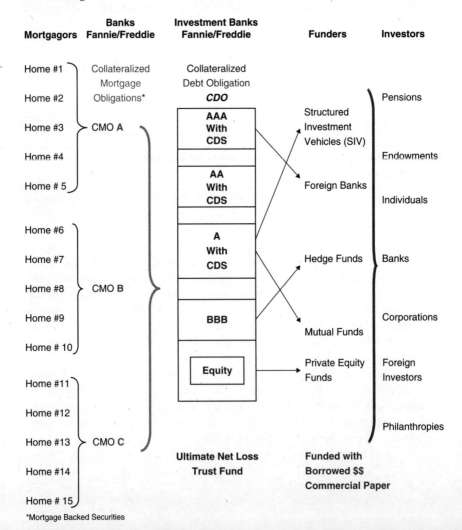

*Mortgage Backed Securities

The consideration of these securities gives insight into the interrelationships of the different segments of the financial markets. Investment banks may acquire mortgage-backed securities (collateralized mortgage obligations) from commercial banks, thrift banks, or government agencies such as "Fannie Mae" and "Freddie Mac." In order to pay for these securities the investment banks may borrow in the money-market sector of the financial markets by issuing "repurchase agreements" or commercial paper. In turn, the investment banks may sell their newly created CDOs (collateralized debt obligations) to affiliated structured investment vehicles or "hedge funds" investment portfolios, or for further sale to investors.

The collateralized debt obligations have themselves been segmented into different tranches (the French word for *slice*) that have different risk characteristics, and therefore different risk premiums. Often to ameliorate the risk, the investment bank that creates the CDO may attach a credit default swap (a CDS can be viewed as a form of insurance) to different segments so as to make them more attractive to investors.

As an exercise, teams of students should array themselves in these financial markets in the roles indicated in the schematic. They should gather a sample group of mortgages from different geographical regions and with different credit qualities and price ranges. The web site of the Mortgage Bankers Association offers real-world data on mortgage delinquency and default rates. Using this data, the teams should evaluate the risk premiums that would be appropriate for a Collateralized Debt Obligation structured with their mortgages.

How Are Equilibrium Prices Discovered in a Competitive Market?

Solving for an equilibrium price using an economic model of a competitive market is one thing; actually discovering an equilibrium value in a real-world, nonfrictionless environment is another matter. In the highly stylized competitive market, the intersection of a demand curve and a supply curve identifies the equilibrium price. In an actual market, transaction prices are set by the interaction of buy and sell orders, and while economic forces might push transaction prices towards equilibrium values, there is no guarantee that an equilibrium will be attained quickly and then closely adhered to. After all, no one actually sees the demand and supply curves, and no one actually knows exactly what the equilibrium value is. The problem of finding equilibrium values is apparent in the equity markets, and it is to these markets that we once again turned to gain insight into this important economic activity.

The chapter has presented price discovery as a critically important economic function of an equity exchange, and it has identified imperfect (or "noisy") price discovery as a cause of market failure. In this application section, we devote further thought to the processes by which prices are set in an actual equities market.* We structure the analysis as follows:

- Assume a large-cap, highly liquid stock that has a sizable number of shareholders.
- Assume that participant orders to buy and to sell shares of that stock are all sent to one equity market, "the exchange."
- Let each participant trade just one round lot of the stock as either a buyer or a seller.
- Consider an environment where analyst expectations are homogeneous, but for the most part assume that analyst expectations are divergent.
- Consider call auction trading on the exchange, but for the most part focus on a continuous order driven market that employs a transparent limit order book as its trading platform.
- In the continuous-order driven market, participants arrive one at a time in random sequence. Upon arrival at the market, a participant observes the limit order book and either submits a market order or places his or her own limit order on the book.
- Assume that no informational change occurs during the trading interval. All that happens is that buyers and sellers arrive at the market in random sequence and trade with each other because they have different valuations for the stock.

Here are our questions:

1. How applicable do you believe the perfectly competitive model is to the market that we are analyzing (a highly liquid, large-cap stock that is traded only on one exchange)?
2. Where do you believe price discovery would take place for the large-cap stock if all relevant information concerning the stock is publicly known, and if all informed participants interpret the information in the same way (that is, form homogeneous expectations): (1) in the upstairs offices of the research analysts, or (2) in the stock exchange where customer buy and sell orders meet and are turned into trades?

---

*Material in this application section draws from Puneet Handa, Robert A. Schwartz, and Ashish Tiwari, "Quote Setting and Price Formation in an Order Driven Market," *Journal of Financial Markets*, 6 (2003), 461–489; and from Jacob Paroush, Robert A. Schwarz, and Avner Wolf, "The Dynamic Process of Price Discovery in an Equity Market," working paper (2009).

3. As a follow-up to question 2, where do you believe price discovery would take place if all informed participants do not interpret information identically (that is, have divergent expectations)?

4. We can represent divergent expectations by assuming just two valuations. With reference to the dividend discount model that we used in the chapter to show the effect of growth rate expectations on stock price, assume that the relatively bullish participants are expecting an annual growth rate of 7.545 percent and are valuing the stock at $55, while the relatively bearish participants are expecting an annual growth rate of 7.000 percent and are valuing the stock at $45. Are you comfortable with this simple representation of divergent expectations?

5. Regarding the two prices mentioned in point 4 ($55 and $45): Are they equilibrium values, or reservation prices, or what?

6. Assume N participants, k percent of whom are bullish (and $1-k$ percent of whom are bearish). Let $k = .75$. Assume the exchange offers call auction trading only, and that the participants' orders reflect their share valuations ($55 and $45). Should an investor submit a buy order at $55 if that is his or her assessment (or a sell order at $45 if that is his or her assessment) when sending an order to a call auction? To answer this one, you might want to refer back to Chapter 4 and the discussion surrounding Exhibit 4.8.

7. As a follow-up to question 6, plot the aggregate market buy and sell curves that have been submitted to the call. Is the equilibrium price uniquely determinate? If not, how do you suggest that the market clearing price be set?

8. Next switch gears and consider a continuous order driven market. We dealt with this case in Chapter 4 and can pick up here where we left off there. In brief, the optimal bid prices that will be set by the bullish participants, and the optimal ask prices that will be set by the bearish participants can be solved for if k (the percentage that is bullish) is known. If $k = 0.5$, the quotes will straddle $50, the average of the two valuations. If $k > 0.5$, the quotes will be closer to $55, the higher valuation. If $k < 0.5$, the quotes will be closer to $45, the lower valuation. Does this make intuitive sense to you?

9. Obtaining the equilibrium noted in point 8 involves solving a set of simultaneous equations. In doing this, we assume not only that all participants know k, but that they all also know how everyone else will act, and that they all know that everybody knows all of this (the so-called "common knowledge" assumption). Consequently, all buyers come up with the same optimal solution for the price of their buy limits orders and whether to instead place a market buy order. Similarly, all sellers

come up with the same optimal solution for the price of their sell limit orders and whether to instead place a market sell order. In this setting, will there be any reason for the quotes to change over the course of the trading period as the buyers and sellers arrive in random sequence?

10. Continuing with the continuous-order driven market, for any given set of valuations (such as $55 and $45), in which of the following three cases is the divergence of expectations the greatest: $k = 0.50$, $k = 0.75$, or $k = 1.00$ (or, equivalently, $k = 0.50$, $k = 0.25$, or $k = 0.00$)?

11. Continuing with the continuous-order driven market, how will the market clear? This is a tricky one. Perhaps $k = .75$. Then there are .75N participants seeking to buy one round lot, and .25N participants seeking to sell one round lot. Even if all of the bearish participants succeed in selling their one round lot, .50N buy orders will not be filled. And yet, given the quotes in the marketplace (which, we remind you, are strictly below the $55 that the buyers would just be willing to pay if they had to), no explicit rationing mechanism is needed and no buyer will feel slighted. How come? What enables the market to clear? (Hint: Think of the willingness of a limit order trader to accept the risk of not executing for the possibility of achieving an execution at a better price.)

12. And now for three big realities: (1) k is not observable before the start of a trading session; (2) participants gain knowledge of k as they see buy and sell orders arriving at the market; and (3) participants can change their valuations while trading progresses and they learn the evaluations of others. That is, if the value of k is revealed to be relatively high, some participants will change their valuations from $45 to $55, and if the value of k is revealed to be relatively low, some other participants will change their valuations from $55 to $45. These three realities give rise to the following questions:

   ■ What does this adaptive valuation behavior imply about the path that prices might follow in the process of attaining a stable equilibrium value?

   ■ Do you see why the current formulation implies that the value a price can converge on is path dependent?

   ■ What does the path dependent process imply about momentum trading?

   ■ The application at the end of Chapter 3 dealt with bandwagon and snob effects. How does this relate to the current formulation?

   ■ Can you sense intuitively that the process that we have described can explain elevated levels of intraday volatility, especially around market openings?

ADDITIONAL READINGS

Becker, Gary, and Kevin Murphy. *Social Economics*. Cambridge, MA: Belknap/Harvard, 2000.

> An analytic framework for measuring how choice permits the optimization of the consumer's utility function.

Chandler, Alfred. *The Visible Hand: The Managerial Revolution in American Business*. Cambridge, MA: Belknap/Harvard, 1977.

> Pulitzer Prize–winning discussion of the evolution of American managerial capitalism and its reliance on market price valuations.

Greenspan, Alan. *The Age of Turbulence*. New York: Penguin, 2008.

> Commentary of the recent Federal Reserve Chairman as to the importance of markets in economic governance.

Irwin, Douglas. *Free Trade under Fire*. Princeton, NJ: Princeton University Press, 2002.

> A discussion of the opening of the world's markets and the resultant efficiencies, with the arguments in favor of and opposed to such open markets.

ANSWERS TO REVIEW QUESTIONS

1. c
2. b
3. b
4. d
5. c
6. b
7. d
8. c
9. a
10. b
11. b
12. c
13. d
14. a
15. b

Public Policy and the Interplay between Competition, Technology, and Regulation

LEARNING OBJECTIVES

■ **Understand public policy concerning a government's involvement in the operations of the micro markets:** Three forces shape the operations of the micro markets: competition, technology development, and regulation. Chapter 7 of *Micro Markets* deals with competition, and Chapter 8 focuses on technology and regulation. You should gain a more precise knowledge of the positives and the negatives for each of these three powerful forces. The free market is far from perfectly efficient, and the inefficiencies of a free market would seemingly call for government regulatory intervention. But government intervention itself can have unintended and undesirable consequences and, as the saying goes, "the cure can be worse than the disease." A major learning objective is to sharpen your thoughts regarding the debates about government's role in regulating markets.

■ **Understand corporate governance structure and self-regulation:** Not all regulation comes from a governmental regulatory body—firms and markets can self-regulate. Self-regulation is a governance structure whereby a firm as a civil institution sets its own rules of organization and operations. The operations of a self-regulatory organization (SRO) depend in part on a firm's governance structure (i.e., whether it is a for-profit organization that is run for the benefit of its shareholders, or a nonprofit, mutual organization that is run for its members). Markets and firms alike require a regulatory structure (a set of rules and regulations). Stock exchanges are among the most regulated of the micro markets, and their rule books largely define their market structures. The specific learning objective here is to understand organizational structure and SRO obligations as they apply to exchanges; this understanding will provide a good platform for considering a federal government's broader involvement in the operations of the micro markets.

- **Appreciate the role that technology and automation play in the evolution of markets.** Markets are impacted by the evolution of invention, innovation, and automation. Together these advances provide for increases in speed and capacity, for the introduction of new production techniques and products, and for the faster dissemination and processing of complex information. In recent decades, technology change and automation have had far-reaching, pervasive effects on micro markets in general, and on securities markets in particular. Along with taking a broad view of these developments, the chapter offers a more focused look at how information technology has affected equity trading (in discussing this, the chapter hones in on the reengineering of the NASDAQ stock market in particular). You should see and appreciate the extent to which a market's structure and operations can be thoroughly transformed by technology change.

- **Be familiar with the evolving regulatory focus.** A government regulatory agency forms its priorities based on its experience, and in conformance with the legislative mandates and directives that it has been given. If the regulatory agenda is unresponsive to the realities of competition and to advances in technology, regulation itself can become a source of market failure. Over the years, regulatory focus has evolved from just maintaining honest markets to include the efficiency of the market for broker/dealer services. More recently it has expanded to also encompass efficiency with regard to the pricing of shares traded.

- **Understand why government regulatory intervention can itself be flawed.** Chapter 7 of *Micro Markets* set forth reasons why private markets may fail to deliver socially desirable outcomes. Chapter 8 sets forth six classic reasons why a government's regulatory intervention may itself be flawed.

- **Assess the effectiveness of a number of specific regulatory initiatives regarding the U.S. equity markets.** The learning objective here is threefold: (1) gain familiarity with U.S. regulatory history concerning the securities markets, (2) see how microeconomic analysis has been applied to these regulatory issues, and (3) consider the efficacy of government regulatory involvement in the context of several concrete issues (to complement a broader but more abstract discussion).

- **Be aware of several caveats concerning government regulatory intervention.** *Micro Markets* analyzes inefficiencies that characterize both private markets and government regulatory intervention. Clearly, regulation is needed. As we have noted, an appropriate structure of rules and regulations is absolutely essential for the proper workings of the private markets. But where should the line be drawn concerning the extent of regulatory intervention? The chapter states that " . . . the vibrancy of competition and the ineffectiveness of competition combine to make good public policy extremely difficult to formulate. For those who would like to see government play an active role we offer the following caveats." The importance of honoring these caveats should be underscored.

CHAPTER SUMMARY

Public policy issues pertaining to the operations of micro markets evolve as the markets respond to three powerful forces: competition, technology, and regulation. We focused on competition in Chapter 6, and in Chapter 7 considered conditions under which competitive micro markets will fail to deliver socially desirable results. Government regulation, a topic that naturally follows from the material in Chapter 7, is the number-one topic for this chapter. In dealing with it, we first considered three integrally related issues: governance structure, a firm's self-regulatory obligations, and technology. Throughout, we paid particular attention to securities markets. These markets are complex, they are of great importance to the broad economy, and they provide a rich opportunity to address a spectrum of public policy issues in a relatively concrete fashion rather than in more abstract terms. Here are the 18 highlights.

1. Regulation of the markets has four major targets. First and foremost is the enforcement of honest behavior. Simply put, trust is of overriding importance; without it, market quality is at best undermined and, at worst, a market may actually collapse. The second target is the quality of free-market outcomes, because the prices and quantities established in an unregulated market may be deemed undesirable from a public policy perspective. Macroeconomic policy is the third target, with monetary and fiscal policy being the primary macroeconomic tools. Fourth is the regulation of market structure. For over three decades in the United States, the structure of the equity markets has been subjected to government regulation and, as has been our way throughout this book, it is to these markets that we have directed our attention.

2. One of the first things to understand about a micro market is its governance structure. In recent years, many securities exchanges around the globe have changed from not-for-profit membership organizations

to being privatized, for-profit companies. In reviewing this development, we considered the customers of an exchange (are they its members or the public traders?), the operations of an exchange (does it provide a service to its members, or does it run a trading platform?), the dynamic development of exchange facilities (are these growth efficient, or is innovation being stymied by technological inertia?), the provision of public goods–type services (including price discovery, liquidity creation, and the tempering of accentuated intraday price volatility), and the branding of a market such as the New York Stock Exchange (as provided by its trading floor and self-regulatory operations).

3. Stock exchanges are typically among the most regulated of the micro markets. They operate within the context of basic rules, common practices, and regulation that is self-established and/or externally imposed. When it sets, supervises, and enforces its own rules, an exchange is a *self-regulatory organization* (SRO). The overall objectives of exchange rules and regulations are investor protection, system protection, and the achievement of a market that is fair and orderly.

4. The delegation to an exchange of the power to set its own rules and regulations is usually stated in a national or federal law. When an exchange establishes its own rules, approval by a national or federal securities commission is usually required. Ideally, government-regulation and self-regulation should complement rather than conflict with each other.

5. Involving people who are closest to the action in rule-making has advantages in terms of knowledge and speed (the rapidity with which decisions can be made and implemented), and self-regulation facilitates realizing these benefits. The negatives include the possibility of competition being impaired by cartelized practices, by weaker players being placed at an unfair disadvantage, and by regulatory capture that happens when stronger players sway the regulatory process.

6. For the past several decades, technology development has transformed many micro markets in general and the equity markets in particular. We reviewed some of these developments, paying particular attention to the NASDAQ Stock Market in the United States, a market that has pioneered the introduction of electronic technology and that has totally reengineered itself by its technology innovations.

7. We noted the far-reaching consequences that technology development and automation have had for employment opportunities, consumption decisions, productivity, economic growth, and the quality of life. While many of the benefits are self-evident, we stressed that technology itself is neutral, that technology is a tool which enables tasks to be

accomplished, and that technology's social desirability depends on the tasks to which it is put and on how the tool is used.

8. Automation has had an extensive impact throughout the securities markets:

- The rapid calculation of price indices has supported the trading of new financial products (e.g., index futures and options), and has provided valuable pricing guides for individual shares.
- Automated trading provides for a faster, more error-free transmission of trade data into post-trade clearance and settlement, has facilitated the overview and regulation of trading, and has been a boon for industry analysts and academic research.
- The speed with which events happen in an electronic marketplace (along with the practice of "slicing and dicing") has led to the use of automated order-writing and submission. The procedure, known as *algorithmic trading*, is not just a product of automation; it is also a symptom of the complexities that electronic trading can introduce.

9. Automation has posed new challenges for equity trading. Unresolved issues persist concerning the electronic handling of large, institutional-sized orders, and the computerized trading of relatively illiquid mid- and small-cap stocks. Trading itself is a challenging application to automate, as the software that makes an electronic market operational has to be specified in far greater detail than is required for human intermediated trading. Moreover, software has to be rewritten to implement any new market structure change (market structure can evolve a good deal more flexibly in a human intermediated environment).

10. As technology transforms economic processes and in so doing alters the distribution of wealth and power across economic agents, regulatory intervention must be reshaped to keep up with the evolving dynamics of the micro markets.

11. The chapter has dealt with the evolving focus of government regulators, going back in the United States to the Congressional Securities Acts Amendments of 1975 (which precluded any return to fixed commissions and mandated the development of a National Market System). In the years that followed, extensive regulatory change has been experienced on both sides of the Atlantic, as government has become far more involved in the structure of the equity markets.

12. We considered in further detail three major regulatory goals:
    1. Assure an honest market.
    2. Assure an efficient provision and pricing of broker/dealer services.
    3. Assure the efficient and reasonably accurate pricing of the shares that are traded.

13. In parallel with our discussion in Chapter 7 of the efficiency (or lack thereof) of free-market competition, we next considered a number of ways in which government regulatory intervention can itself be flawed. Here is the list:
    ■ Inadequate procedural safeguards.
    ■ Existence of jurisdictional disputes.
    ■ Cost to society of regulating markets.
    ■ Cost to the markets of being regulated.
    ■ Incomplete and imperfect knowledge on the part of the regulators.

14. We then switched from an aerial view of the problems concerning government intervention and took a closer look at how the U.S. Congress and the U.S. Securities and Exchange Commission (SEC) has intervened in the structure and operations of the U.S. securities markets. The following regulatory initiatives were discussed:
    ■ The end of fixed commissions as mandated by the Congressional Securities Acts Amendments of 1975.
    ■ The imposition of a best execution obligation (also part of the 1975 Securities Acts Amendments).
    ■ The elimination of off-board trading restrictions (which, in the United States, was accomplished in 2000).
    ■ The implicit collusion case against NASDAQ dealers that had its origin in Christie and Schultz's 1994 landmark paper in the *Journal of Finance*.
    ■ The change to penny pricing in 2001.
    ■ A 2005 SEC release—referred to as Reg NMS—that established an order protection rule that was designed to prevent the execution of trades at inferior prices (the trade-through rule).

15. In the section of the chapter, "Caveats for Public Policy," we raised the question of whether markets, with all of their imperfections, should be left free to evolve naturally, or whether a government agency should participate in designing market structure and in writing the rulebook. Once again we addressed the question, not in the abstract, but with reference to a specific market—the equities market.

    We had the following to say: "Market architecture is highly complex. There is a lot involved about it that students of the market do not understand or agree on. The very measurements of market quality and best execution are subject to considerable ambiguity. Market structure changes have unintended consequences, especially in a rapidly evolving technological environment. And when a government-mandated structural change goes awry, government recognition, understanding, and appropriate corrective action, if ever taken, may not be forthcoming for years."

16. We continued on to say, "The vibrancy of competition and the ineffectiveness of competition combine to make good public policy extremely difficult to formulate. For those who would like to see government play an active role, we offer the following caveats":

   - Government agencies, liking to monitor what they regulate, tend to focus on readily observable aspects of market quality such as bid-ask spreads, and they pay insufficient attention to more amorphous matters such as the accuracy of price discovery.

   - While regulatory authorities are very focused on the exercise of monopoly power, there are other considerations that should be paid more attention to: network externalities, free riding on price discovery, and the nonexplicit components of trading costs such as market impact costs and errors in price discovery.

   - Once government becomes involved in market design, the process tends to become self-perpetuating.

   - Considerable regulatory attention is commonly given to "fairness," to "leveling the playing field." But all participants are not equal, free markets are not necessarily fair, and all too often a firm that is threatened by competitive pressure uses the fairness argument in an appeal for regulatory intervention rather than itself strengthening its position in the market.

   - Vested interests and technological inertia certainly exist. But the regulatory process itself can also stymie innovation, in part because obtaining necessary regulatory approvals is typically a lengthy and difficult process.

   - A marketplace in certain respects is an ecology, and regulation that addresses one facet of a market's operations can have unintended consequences on other parts of the ecological system.

17. The free market does not always effectively deliver the results that we may desire from a public policy point of view, and the free market can be a very harsh master. But nothing is ever close to being perfect, and that includes both the markets themselves and the governments that might regulate them. The public policy issue of deregulation versus reregulation should not be approached solely as an abstract question. Appropriate regulation is certainly needed, but achieving it is not at all easy.

18. We quoted the poet Shelley concerning the power of the west wind both to destroy and to preserve, and ended the chapter with this thought: "Our [final] caveat is that the strengths of the markets be honored, that we do not lose faith in the efficacy of a free market."

GLOSSARY

algorithmic trading   Computer-driven trading. Algos are computer-resident trading rules that electronically generate buy and sell orders.

Buttonwood Tree Agreement   The 1794 agreement that established the New York Stock Exchange.

commission bundling   The provision of additional services (e.g., research reports, data sets, or tickets to a choice sporting event) by brokerage houses that commission revenue pays for.

counterparty risk   The risk that the contraparty to a contract will fail to perform its obligations under that contract. In equity trading, the risk that the contraparty to a trade will not deliver shares (to a buyer) or cash (to a seller).

exchange-traded funds (ETFs)   An investment vehicle that is traded on an exchange, much like ordinary shares. An ETF holds stocks, bonds, or other assets in trust, and shares of the ETF trade at roughly asset value of the underlying assets that comprise the ETF.

fails to deliver   The failure of a seller to deliver securities or cash within a settlement period (usually two days).

over-the-counter (OTC) market   A decentralized market for securities. Participants in an OTC market typically trade with a dealer firm that they communicate with either by telephone or computer. The small-cap, less liquid segment of the broader NASDAQ market.

pennying   The practice of placing a bid one penny above the highest existing bid on the book, or of placing an offer one penny below the lowest existing offer on the book, so as to gain priority over the previously posted orders.

Ponzi scheme   A fraud in which an investment company uses funds from new investors to pay preexisting investors. Also known as a pyramid scheme.

price discovery   In any micro market, price discovery is the process of finding an equilibrium value for a good, service, or productive resource that is being traded. Price discovery is a complex, imperfect process when participants do not simultaneously reveal their complete demand and supply functions. In an equity market, price discovery is the dynamic process of finding a value that best reflects the broad market's desire to hold shares of a stock. In equity markets, price discovery occurs most prominently after the receipt of news and following market openings as prices adjust to new economic conditions and to changes in the investors' desires to hold shares.

regulations   Rules established by external, government regulators.

regulatory arbitrage   A regulated firm exploiting competing regulators so as to obtain the most favorable regulatory oversight.

regulatory lag   A delayed regulatory response to innovation, technological change, changing economic circumstances, or any other development affecting a micro market, or a delayed regulatory response to an industry request for regulatory approval for new rules or facility.

rules   Uniform and standard practices and methods typically established by an SRO, and formally approved by the overseeing government regulator.

self-regulatory organization (SRO)   A nongovernment regulatory entity that establishes and enforces rules of conduct for a firm or industry group that it has responsibility for.

CURRENT EVENTS DISCUSSIONS

1. Should Markets Be Allowed to "Collapse," or Should Government Intervene?

In the late summer of 2008, after struggling for over a year with the illiquidity of the American financial markets, and particularly the "money markets," the government of the United States through its Treasury Department and its central bank, the Federal Reserve System, sought to stabilize the financial markets. In a short period of less than two weeks, the government took the following actions:

- Seized and guaranteed the debt of the primary mortgage-lending entities, the Federal National Mortgage Association (Fannie Mae) and The Federal Home Loan Mortgage Corporation (Freddie Mac).
- Guaranteed approximately $35 billion of the debt of the largest U.S. insurance enterprise, the American International Group (AIG).
- Refused to provide financial support to the third-largest U.S. investment bank, Lehman Brothers; this led to Lehman Brothers's bankruptcy, which further aggravated the illiquidity of the "money markets."
- Promoted and assisted the acquisition of the largest American broker-dealer firm, Merrill Lynch, by the largest U.S. commercial bank, Bank of America.
- Proposed and submitted to Congress a $700 billion financial assistance program for the 9,000 private U.S. banks.

These actions were the largest intervention ever on the part of any government into the public financial markets. In that the financial institutions are privately owned firms and the several affected markets were "self-regulating," the governments' actions were unusual and largely unprecedented. In consequence, most commentators suggested that these actions on the part of the government to "stabilize" the financial markets raised fundamental questions as to the efficacy and reliability of "free markets."

The below is an extract from a lengthy article from the *Wall Street Journal* some three months after the crucial events of late summer 2008.

The Weekend That Wall Street Died

Ties That Long United Strongest Firms Unraveled as Lehman Sank Toward Failure: Implosion of an Industry

With his investment bank facing a near-certain failure, Lehman Brothers Holdings Inc.'s chief executive officer, Richard Fuld Jr., placed yet another phone call to the man he thought could save him. The titans of Wall Street faced the biggest gambles of their professional lives this year—and blundered to varying degrees. Read how these executives misjudged dangers facing their institutions and financial markets. Mr. Fuld was already effectively out of options by the afternoon of Sunday, Sept. 14. The U.S. government said it wouldn't fund a bailout for Lehman, the country's oldest investment bank. Britain's Barclays PLC had agreed in principle to buy the loss-wracked firm, but the deal fell apart. Bank of America Corp., initially seen as Lehman's most likely buyer, had said two days earlier that it couldn't do a deal without federal aid—and by Sunday was deep in secret negotiations to take over Lehman rival Merrill Lynch & Co.

Desperate to avoid steering his 25,000-person company into bankruptcy proceedings, Mr. Fuld dialed the Charlotte, N.C., home of Bank of America Chairman Kenneth D. Lewis. His calls so far that weekend had gone unreturned. This time, Mr. Lewis's wife, Donna, again picked up, and told the boss of Lehman Brothers: If Mr. Lewis wanted to call back, he would call back. Mr. Fuld paused, then apologized for bothering her. "I am so sorry," he said.

His lament could also have been for the investment-banking model that had come to embody the words "Wall Street." Within hours of his call, Lehman announced it would file for bankruptcy protection. Within a week, Wall Street as it was known—loosely regulated, daringly risky and lavishly rewarded—was dead.

As Mr. Fuld waged his increasingly desperate bid to save his firm that weekend, the bosses of Wall Street's other three giant investment banks were locked in their own battles as their firms came under mounting pressure. It was a weekend unlike anything Wall Street had ever seen: In past crises, its bosses had banded together to save their way of life. This time, the financial hole they had dug for themselves was too deep. It was every man for himself, and Mr. Fuld, who declined to comment for this article, was the odd man out.

For the U.S. securities industry to unravel as spectacularly as it did in September, many parties had to pull on many threads. Mortgage bankers gave loans to Americans for homes they couldn't

afford. Investment houses packaged these loans into complex instruments whose risk they didn't always understand. Ratings agencies often gave their seal of approval, investors borrowed heavily to buy, regulators missed the warning signs. But at the center of it all—and paid hundreds of millions of dollars during the boom to manage their firms' risk—were the four bosses of Wall Street.

Morgan Stanley's CEO, John Mack, told shareholders the U.S. subprime crisis was in the eighth or ninth inning. The same month, Goldman Sachs Group Inc.'s chief executive, Lloyd Blankfein, said, "We're probably in the third or fourth quarter" of a four-quarter game.

Messrs. Mack and Blankfein had some reason to be confident. Mr. Mack had been late to steer Morgan into mortgage trading, and relatively early to sell assets and raise cash. Goldman, under Mr. Blankfein, had even less direct exposure to subprime investments. Mr. Blankfein also took comfort in a stockpile of government bonds and other securities his firm held in case it ran into deep funding problems. By the second quarter, Goldman had increased this store of funds more than 30% from earlier in the year, to $88 billion. John Thain, a former Goldman Sachs president and New York Stock Exchange head, had arrived at Merrill Lynch in December 2007.

Problems were more acute at Merrill Lynch and Lehman.

Lehman, now the smallest of the major Wall Street firms, also faced billions of dollars in write-downs from bad mortgage-related investments. In June, Lehman reported the first quarterly loss in its 14 years as a public company. Under Mr. Fuld, Lehman raised capital. But critics say Mr. Fuld was slow to shed bad assets and profitable lines of business. He pushed for better terms with at least one investor that ended up driving it away.

Mr. Fuld had faced challenges to his firm before. Since taking Lehman's reins in 1994, he expanded the 158-year-old bond house into lucrative areas such as investment banking and stock trading. Over the years, he had tamped unfounded rumors about the firm's health and vowed to remain independent. "As long as I am alive this firm will never be sold," Mr. Fuld said in December 2007, according to a person who spoke with him then. "And if it is sold after I die, I will reach back from the grave and prevent it."

In the summer of 2008, Mr. Fuld remained confident, particularly given the security of the Fed's discount window. "We have access to Fed funds," Mr. Fuld told executives at the time. "We can't fail now." By Friday, Sept. 12, failure appeared to be an option for Lehman.

Over that week, confidence in Lehman plunged. The firm said its third-quarter losses could total almost $4 billion. Lehman's clearing bank, J.P. Morgan, wanted an extra $5 billion in collateral. Lehman's attempts to raise money from a Korean bank had stalled. Credit agencies were warning that if Lehman didn't raise more capital over the weekend, it could face a downgrade. That would likely force the firm to put up more collateral for its outstanding loans and increase its costs for new loans.

If Mr. Fuld couldn't find an investor for Lehman by Sunday night, the fiercely independent boss could be forced to steer his firm into bankruptcy proceedings.

Earlier that week, Mr. Fuld had approached Bank of America's Mr. Lewis about buying Lehman. A U.S. Treasury official, meanwhile, had contacted Barclays of Britain to suggest it consider taking a stake in Lehman. Mr. Fuld's top executives spent Friday shuttling between the two suitors' law firms.

In a Merrill Lynch conference room in downtown Manhattan that morning, Mr. Thain was on a call with Merrill's board of directors, discussing how to address the chaos. "Lehman is going down, and the [short sellers] are coming after us next," warned Merrill director John Finnegan. "Tell me how this story is going to end differently."

Merrill would be fine, Mr. Thain said. "We are not Lehman," he responded.

Soon after, Mr. Thain gathered along with Morgan's Mr. Mack and Goldman's Mr. Blankfein at the New York Federal Reserve in downtown Manhattan, in a room once used to cash coupons on Treasury bills. The three men were greeted by the masters of the world's biggest economy—Federal Reserve Chairman Ben Bernanke, Treasury Secretary Henry Paulson, New York Fed Chief Timothy Geithner and Securities and Exchange Commission chief Christopher Cox. It was a signal moment for the Wall Street firms, which after years of being monitored by the SEC would all soon come under the regulatory watch of a newly powerful Fed.

The federal officials told the Wall Street chiefs to return in the morning. If the mess at Lehman could be fixed, it would be the job of the Wall Street bosses. There would be no public bailout.

Mr. Thain's black SUV pulled up in front of the New York Fed just before 8 a.m. Top executives from all four investment banks—minus Lehman's Mr. Fuld—were there. Federal officials broke Messrs. Thain, Mack and Blankfein and their top aides into groups. One studied the potential fallout from a Lehman failure. Another was charged with putting a value on Lehman's controversial real-estate investments. A third group, which included Mr. Thain and Morgan's Mr. Mack, was supposed to discuss an industry-led bailout for Lehman.

Mr. Mack questioned Wall Street's ability to repair markets. The firms could try to backstop Lehman, he argued, but there was no guarantee they wouldn't have to rescue another rival later. "If we're going to do this deal, where does it end?" he said. As Mr. McDade discussed Lehman's position, Mr. Thain had an epiphany: "This could be me sitting here next Friday." Mr. Thain pushed his chair back and left the group to caucus with top Merrill officers. "Lehman is not going to make it," he told them. Mr. Thain stepped to a sidewalk behind the New York Fed and called the Bank of America chief at his home in Charlotte. "I can be there in a few hours," Mr. Lewis said.

Merrill's talks with Bank of America, however, were on track at the bank's law firm, Wachtell Lipton. Merrill's team was camped out on Wachtell's 34th floor. Bank of America's team was on the 33rd. Around midnight, Mr. Lewis left the law firm for his apartment in the Time Warner Center. Pizza arrived at Wachtell at 3 a.m.

At 9 a.m., Sunday the chiefs of finance arrived again at the New York Fed for a second day of meetings. By the time Mr. Thain arrived, the Merrill chief had a number of options in his back pocket. Rolling up to the meetings at around the same time was Goldman's chief, Mr. Blankfein. A Goldman aide, referring to days of meltdowns and meetings, carped to Mr. Blankfein: "I don't think I can take another day of this." Mr. Blankfein retorted: "You're getting out of a Mercedes to go to the New York Federal Reserve—you're not getting out of a Higgins boat on Omaha Beach."

By mid-afternoon, word emerged that Bank of America was in talks with Merrill Lynch. Mr. Cohen, the attorney, broke the news to Mr. Fuld. "I guess this confirms our worst fears," Mr. Fuld said.

A more somber scene was playing out at Lehman. Directors, who had been camped at the Midtown offices all day, gathered at around 8 p.m. in the firm's board room. Weil lawyers and Lehman executives summarized the Fed meeting to the frustrated board. One of Mr. Fuld's assistants broke in to hand him a note: The SEC chairman wanted to address Lehman's board by speakerphone.

Mr. Cox, criticized for his allegedly minor role in the government's bailout of Bear Stearns, had been reluctant to call

Lehman. The SEC chief finally called from the New York Fed, surrounded by several staffers, at the urging of Mr. Paulson, the Treasury secretary. "This is serious," said Mr. Cox. "The board has a grave matter before it," he said. John D. McComber, a former president of the Export-Import Bank and a Lehman director for 14 years, asked: "Are you directing us to authorize" a bankruptcy filing? The SEC chief muted his phone. A minute later, he came back on the line. "You have a grave responsibility and you need to act accordingly," he replied. As the meeting wrapped up around 10 p.m., Mr. Fuld, his suit jacket now off, leaned back in his chair. "I guess this is goodbye," he said. Lehman would file about four hours later.

Rather than soothing markets, Lehman's bankruptcy filing roiled them—slamming trading partners that had direct exposure to the firm and sowing fears that Wall Street's remaining giants weren't safe from failure. Shares of Morgan and Goldman plunged. In the credit-default swap market, the price of insurance against defaults of Morgan and Goldman soared.

Hedge funds sought to withdraw more than $100 billion in assets from Morgan Stanley. The firm's clearing bank, Bank of New York Mellon, wanted an extra $4 billion in collateral.

By Thursday, Fed officials were urging Morgan to become a commercial bank. Such a move would require Morgan to scale back its bets with borrowed money, run the risk of selling lucrative business lines and accept new onsite regulation from the Fed. After 139 years as a securities firm, Goldman, too, would also reshape itself as a commercial bank. Within hours, the era of Wall Street's giants was over.

—Susanne Craig, Jeffrey McCracken, Aaron Lucchetti,
and Kate Kelly, *Wall Street Journal* (December 29, 2008)

Questions

1. As the financial crisis of 2007–2009 evolved, the federal government was increasingly drawn into the turmoil with the Treasury Department, the Federal Reserve System, the Federal Deposit Insurance Corporation, the SEC, the Congress, and several other agencies playing increasingly larger roles. Compounding the government's involvement was a presidential election in November 2008 and the subsequent inauguration of a new administration in January 2009. As a consequence, many of the government actions were motivated by political rather than economic purposes. The preceding article describes the events of September 2008

which in turn led to further events in the emerging financial crisis. For a class discussion of the efficacy of government intervention in free markets, select a firm that was a major "player" in the emerging crisis, research its performance, and be prepared to present your interpretation of its conduct.

2. In the emerging financial crisis, the merger of Merrill Lynch into Bank of America was subsequently viewed as problematical, leading to the "firing" of John Thain. The immediate issue of his termination was certain incentive compensation "bonuses" paid to officers of Merrill Lynch. As the executive compensation expert consulted by Mr. Lewis of Bank of America, what would be your recommendation concerning these 2008 bonuses and future bonuses to the former officers of Merrill Lynch? Mr. Lewis wants your recommendation tomorrow.

What Obligation Do Regulators Have to "Police" Markets in Detecting and Preventing Criminal Behavior?

All free markets have the economic function of allocating scarce economic resources among competing users. In that substantial risks and rewards attend the operation of free markets, the human tendency to seek the rewards without bearing the risks is well illustrated in the history of all markets. In our discussion of "market failure," we have noted both the importance of the assurance of honesty and the regulatory impulses to enforce rules to obtain that assurance. The American financial markets have recently witnessed one of their more egregious incidents of the failure of honesty in the episode of the Bernard Madoff Investment enterprise. While it has been characterized as a "Ponzi" scheme, there are several aspects to the episode, which go beyond mere fraud and raise serious questions about the regulatory efficacy of both government and self-regulatory entities.

The following article from the London *Economist* summarizes these various aspects.

The Madoff Affair

Con of the Century

There are no heroes in the Madoff story; only villains and suckers.

Bernard Madoff worked as a lifeguard to earn enough money to start his own securities firm. Almost half a century later, the colossal Ponzi scheme into which it mutated has proved impossible to keep afloat.

The $17.1 billion that Mr Madoff claimed to have under management earlier this year is all but gone. His alleged confession that the fraud could top $50 billion looks increasingly plausible: clients have admitted to exposures amounting to more than half that. On December 16th the head of the Securities Investor Protection Corporation, which is recovering what it can for investors, said the multiple sets of accounts kept by the 70-year-old were in "complete disarray" and could take six months to sort out. It is hard to imagine a more apt end to Wall Street's worst year in decades.

The known list of victims grows longer and more star-studded by the day. Among them are prominent billionaires, including Steven Spielberg; the owner of the New York Mets baseball team; Carl Shapiro, a nonagenarian clothing magnate who may have lost $545m; thousands of wealthy retirees; and a cluster of mostly Jewish charities, some of which face closure. Dozens of supposedly sophisticated financial firms were caught out too, including banks such as Santander and HSBC, and Fairfield Greenwich, an alternative-investment specialist that had funnelled no less than $7.5 billion to Mr Madoff.

Though his operation resembled a hedge-fund shop, he was in fact managing client money in brokerage accounts within his firm, seemingly as Merrill Lynch or Smith Barney would. A lot of this came from funds of funds, which invest in pools of hedge funds, and was channelled to Mr Madoff via "feeder funds" with which he had special relationships. Some banks, such as the Dutch arm of Fortis, lent heavily to funds of funds that wanted to invest.

On the face of it, the attractions were clear. Mr Madoff's pedigree was top-notch: a pioneering market-maker, he had chaired NASDAQ, had advised the government on market issues and was a noted philanthropist. Turning away some investors and telling those he accepted not to talk to outsiders produced a sense of exclusivity. He generated returns to match: in the vicinity of 10% a year, through thick and thin.

That last attraction should also have served as a warning; the results were suspiciously smooth. Mr Madoff barely ever suffered a down month, even in choppy markets (he was up in November, as the S&P index tumbled 7.5%). He allegedly has now confessed that this was achieved by creating a pyramid scheme in which existing clients' returns were topped up, as needed, with money from new investors.

He claimed to be employing an investment strategy known as "split-strike conversion". This is a fairly common approach that entails buying and selling different sorts of options to reduce volatility. But those who bothered to look closely had doubts. Aksia, an advisory firm, concluded that the S&P 100 options market that Mr Madoff claimed to trade was far too small to handle a portfolio of his size. It advised its clients not to invest. So did MPI, a quantitative-research firm, after an analysis in 2006 failed to find a legitimate strategy that matched his returns—though they were closely correlated with those of Bayou, a fraudulent hedge fund that had collapsed a year earlier.

This was not the only danger signal. Stock holdings were liquidated every quarter, presumably to avoid reporting big positions. For a godfather of electronic trading, Mr Madoff ran the business along antediluvian lines: clients and feeder-fund managers were denied online access to their accounts. Even more worryingly, he cleared his own trades, with no external custodian. They were audited, of course, but by a tiny firm with three employees, one of whom was a secretary and another an 80-year-old based in Florida.

Perhaps the biggest warning sign was the secrecy with which the investment business was conducted. It was a black box, run by a tiny team at a very long arm's length from the group's much bigger broker-dealer. Clients too were kept in the dark. They seemed not to mind as long as the returns remained strong, accepting that to ask Bernie to reveal his strategy would be as crass as demanding to see Coca-Cola's magic formula. Mr Madoff reinforced the message by occasionally ejecting a client who asked awkward questions.

This failure of due diligence by so many funds of funds will deal the industry a blow. They are paid to screen managers, to pick the best and to diversify clients' holdings—none of which they did properly in this case. Some investors are understandably irate that their funds—including one run by the chairman of GMAC, a troubled car-loan firm—charged above-average fees, only to plonk the bulk of their cash in Mr Madoff's lap. This is the last thing hedge funds need, plagued as they are by a wave of redemption requests.

Mr Madoff's investment business was overseen by the Securities and Exchange Commission (SEC), but it failed to carry out any examinations despite receiving complaints from investors and rivals since as long ago as the late 1990s. As a Wall Street fixture, Mr Madoff was close to several SEC officials. His niece, the firm's compliance lawyer, even married a former member of the team that had inspected the market-making division's books in 2003—though there is no evidence of impropriety.

In a rare mea culpa, *Christopher Cox, the SEC's chairman, has called its handling of the case "deeply troubling" and promised an investigation of its "multiple failures". Having already been lambasted for fiddling while investment banks burned, the commission is now likelier than ever to be restructured, or perhaps even dismantled, in the regulatory overhaul expected under Barack Obama. As* The Economist *went to press Mr Obama was expected to name Mary Schapiro, an experienced brokerage regulator, to replace Mr Cox.*

The rules themselves will need changing, too. All investment managers, not just mutual funds, could now be forced to use external clearing agents to ensure third-party scrutiny, says Larry Harris of the University of Southern California's Marshall School of Business. Regulation of financial firms' accountants may also need tightening. And more could be done to encourage whistle-blowing. Mr Madoff claims to have acted alone. But given the huge amount of paperwork required to keep his scam going, it seems unlikely that no one else knew about it.

Above all, however, investors need to help themselves. This pyramid scheme may have been unprecedented, but the lessons are old ones: spread your eggs around and, as Mr Harris puts it, "investigate your good stories as well as your bad ones." This is particularly true of money managers who work deep in the shadows or seem beyond reproach—even more so during booms, when the temptation to swindle grows along with the propensity to speculate. There will always be "sheep to be shorn", as Charles Kindleberger memorably wrote in "Manias, Panics and Crashes". Let us hope they never again line up in such numbers.
                                   —The Economist *(print edition) (December 18, 2008)*

Question

1. Mr. Madoff was appointed as a special consultant and then as a member of the Security and Exchange Commission's Advisory Board on Market Operations. He held these positions for almost ten years until the exposure of his fraud in December 2008. You have been assigned to research the history of the SEC from its initiation in 1933–1934 through today as a special project for your class. Give special attention to the evolution of the SEC in the period from the mid 1970s through the 1990s, when Mr. Madoff became a consultant. Based on your research, make a determination as to the cause of the Madoff appointment, and what corrective actions should be taken at the SEC.

REVIEW QUESTIONS

1. A self-regulatory organization
   a. Is a government agency.
   b. Sets and enforces its own rules of behavior.
   c. Is a governance structure.
   d. None of the above.
2. A demutualized (privatized) exchange
   a. Seeks to maximize the value of access privileges.
   b. Considers its members rather than investors to be its customers.
   c. Is a profit-maximizing organization.
   d. Is a non-for-profit organization.
3. NASDAQ
   a. Was initially a quotation system of the NASD.
   b. Is an electronic marketplace.
   c. Is a hybrid market that offers both quote-driven and order-driven trading.
   d. All of the above.
4. New information technology
   a. Has transformed trading in global financial markets.
   b. Is easily incorporated into productive processes when shown to increase productivity.
   c. Has paved the way to virtually costless trading.
   d. All of the above.
5. Price discovery refers to
   a. A firm's decision regarding how best to price its products.
   b. The determination of an equilibrium price in an equity market.
   c. A consumer searching for the place that offers the best price for a given product.
   d. None of the above.
6. The primary objectives of a regulatory authority with regard to the equity markets should include
   a. Keeping markets fair and honest.
   b. Ensuring that broker/dealer services are reasonably priced.
   c. Enhancing market efficiency with regard to the pricing of shares that are traded.
   d. All of the above.
7. A best-execution obligation was set forth as part of the
   a. 1975 Securities Acts Amendments.
   b. 1933 Glass-Steagall Act.
   c. 1934 Securities and Exchange Act.
   d. None of the above.

8. The New York Stock Exchange's Rule 390
   a. Was an order concentration rule that is no longer in effect.
   b. Required that exchange member firms bring their orders for exchange-listed stocks to an exchange.
   c. Strengthened the NYSE's competitive position in the marketplace.
   d. All of the above.

9. Given the possible need for government action in markets where asymmetric information is an issue, which of the following is a valid concern?
   a. The government almost always has more information than the private parties.
   b. Private markets have no means of dealing with information asymmetries on their own.
   c. The government is itself an imperfect institution.
   d. Legally, the government can rarely intervene in markets.

10. Automation in the equity markets has enabled price indexes (such as the Dow Jones Industrial Average) to be computed with high frequency. This in turn
    a. Has sharpened price discovery for individual shares.
    b. Facilitated the development of the ETF market.
    c. Led to an increased volume of options trading.
    d. All of the above.

11. Which of the following are among the regulatory functions that are necessary for an exchange to operate effectively?
    a. Market surveillance in real time.
    b. Market surveillance post trade.
    c. Overseeing member positions and market risk.
    d. All of the above.

12. Which of the following is an advantage of self-regulation in a dynamic marketplace with quickly evolving technology?
    a. It results in a marketplace's faster, more flexible, and more effective adaptation in a fast-changing environment.
    b. It increases potential for regulatory lag.
    c. It necessarily makes a marketplace a more competitive place.
    d. Both a and b are correct.

13. Which of the following statements about the NYSE and NASDAQ is correct?
    a. Until late 1990s, the NYSE was a primarily a human-intermediated, order-driven (agency) market.
    b. Until late 1990s, NASDAQ was a primarily quote-driven (competitive dealer) market.
    c. Presently, NASDAQ is no longer a predominantly quote-driven market and currently the NYSE operates an electronic, order-driven platform.
    d. All of the above.

14. The accuracy of prices discovered in the major market centers is important for a variety of reasons, including which of the following?
    a. Such prices signal information to traders and are used for marking-to-market.
    b. Such prices are used in the calculation of margin requirements.
    c. Such prices are used for price-basing in related markets.
    d. All of the above are correct.

15. Which of the statements about a trade-through is FALSE?
    a. It refers to a transaction that occurs at a price that is higher than the best-posted offer or lower than the best-posted bid, and orders at these better prices are not included in the transaction.
    b. 2005 Reg NMS has made it easier for a new trading venue to receive order flow and deliver executions.
    c. Reg NMS has required that strict time priorities be enforced across the various trading venues.
    d. Reg NMS makes an exception for prices set by slower, floor-based markets; such prices can be traded through.

APPLICATIONS AND ISSUES

Thoughts on Government Regulation

1. We started the chapter with the statement that markets around the world are being shaped by three powerful forces: technology, competition, and regulation. For much of the chapter we have focused on the third. From a public policy perspective, appropriate government regulation is certainly needed for the micro markets to operate effectively and yet regulation, unless properly structured, can unduly impair the workings of a free market. Quite clearly, achieving an optimal balance between the competitive forces of a marketplace and regulatory requirements, which are imposed by government, is far from a simple matter. What are your thoughts about this issue? Has your thinking about it been affected by your study of microeconomics? Please explain.

2. Market efficiency was our topic in Chapter 7, and in dealing with it we considered the financial turmoil that hit the United States and world markets in fall 2008. What are your thoughts about the broad causes of the market breakdown and your ideas concerning steps that a government should take to rectify the situation? Has your thinking about this issue been affected by the discussion in Chapter 8? Please explain.

3. Select a nonfinancial micro market that you have some familiarity with that has been subjected to meaningful government regulation. Describe the regulation and the economic justification for having imposed it. Do

any of the causes of market failure that we enumerated in Chapter 7 justify the regulation? What is your opinion about the success of the regulation?

4. We focused in this chapter on six major regulatory initiatives that the U. S. government has taken with regard to the U.S. equity markets, starting with the Securities Acts Amendments of 1975. While the first initiative, the preclusion of fixed commissions, has been broadly acclaimed as a success, we did not come to firm conclusions about the others. Instead, we noted some points of justification, some points of concern, and stressed the complexity of the issues. What is your thinking about the initiatives? You might approach this question by looking at each of them individually, and/or by thinking more broadly about the direction in which they have collectively taken our markets.

5. For equity trading, market quality has to do with the markets being reasonably transparent (can participants get adequate and timely information about market quotes and trades?), reasonably consolidated (is the marketplace concentrated to an extent that raises fear of monopoly power, or is it fragmented to an extent that impairs reasonable price and quantity discovery?), and what is the quality of price discovery? What is your assessment of the U.S. government's regulatory initiatives in light of these market quality goals? Are there any other market quality goals that you think should be taken into account?

Should Regulators Be Held Accountable for Failure to Regulate?

The *Wall Street Journal* article in the earlier section on Current Events Discussions presents the difficult role of Christopher Cox, Chairman of the Securities and Exchange Commission (SEC), in the tense deliberations of that fateful weekend. In that the SEC had, up to that time, the primary responsibility for regulating both the financial industry and the securities exchanges, Cox's actions reflect on the efficacy of government regulation. The consequence of the major investment banks converting into "bank holding companies" was to transfer the regulatory responsibility for the industry from the SEC to the Controller of the Currency, which is a bureau of the Treasury Department.

It would be useful to research and discuss the respective regulatory roles before, during, and after the fateful September of the different government entities, the Treasury Department, the SEC, the Federal Reserve Board, and the Anti-Trust division of the Justice Department.

In our discussions of "honesty" as one of the requisites of free markets, and whether such standards are better enforced and supervised by self-regulating organizations (SROs) or government entities, the discovery of the Ponzi scheme run by Bernard Madoff and his company is illustrative. Here also it would be productive for understanding the efficacy of regulation to consider the regulatory roles of the different government entities, the Treasury Department, the SEC, the Federal Reserve Board, and the Anti-Trust division of the Justice Department. It would also be productive to consider the roles of the different SROs, the New York Stock Exchange, Nasdaq, the Securities Investor Protection Corporation, and Financial Industry Regulatory Authority.

ADDITIONAL READINGS

Buchholz, Todd. *New Ideas from Dead Economists*. New York: Plume/ Penguin, 1999.

   An accessible introduction to the works of the major microeconomic theorists, from Adam Smith to the present.

Council of Economic Advisors. *Economic Report of the President*. U.S. Government Printing Office, Annually.

   The annual report on the performance and prospects for the American economy, and a primary source of economic data.

Galbraith, John K. *Economics and the Public Purpose*. Boston: Houghton Mifflin, 1973.

   The classic commentary of the American "institutionalist" economist, including his critique of market pricing.

Warsh, David. *Knowledge and the Wealth of Nations*. New York: W.W. Norton, 2006.

   A survey discussion of the emergence of knowledge and education as the primary force in microeconomic development.

ANSWERS TO REVIEW QUESTIONS

1. b
2. c
3. d
4. a
5. b
6. d
7. a
8. d
9. c
10. d
11. d
12. a
13. d
14. d
15. c

About the Authors

Robert A. Schwartz is Marvin M. Speiser Professor of Finance and University Distinguished Professor in the Zicklin School of Business, Baruch College, CUNY. Before joining the Baruch faculty in 1997, he was Professor of Finance and Economics and Yamaichi Faculty Fellow at New York University's Leonard N. Stern School of Business, where he had been a member of the faculty since 1965. In 1966, Professor Schwartz received his Ph.D. in Economics from Columbia University. His research is in the area of financial economics, with a primary focus on the structure of securities markets. He has published over 60 refereed journal articles, 12 edited books, and five authored books, including *The Equity Trader Course*, co-authored with Reto Francioni and Bruce Weber (John Wiley & Sons, 2006); *Equity Markets in Action: The Fundamentals of Liquidity, Market Structure and Trading*, co-authored with Reto Francioni (John Wiley & Sons, 2004); and *Reshaping the Equity Markets: A Guide for the 1990s* (Harper Business, 1991; reissued by Business One Irwin, 1993). He has served as a consultant to various market centers including the New York Stock Exchange, the American Stock Exchange, NASDAQ, the London Stock Exchange, Instinet, the Arizona Stock Exchange, Deutsche Börse, and the Bolsa Mexicana. From April 1983 to April 1988, he was an associate editor of the *Journal of Finance*, and he is currently an associate editor of the *Review of Quantitative Finance and Accounting*, and the *Review of Pacific Basin Financial Markets and Policies*, and is a member of the advisory boards of *International Finance* and *The Journal of Trading*. In December 1995, Professor Schwartz was named the first chairman of NASDAQ's Economic Advisory Board, and he served on the EAB until Spring 1999. He is developer, with Bruce Weber and Gregory Sipress, of the trading and market structure simulation, TraderEx (www.etraderex.com/).

Michael G. Carew is Distinguished Lecturer and Associate Professor of Economics at Baruch College of the City University of New York. He received his PhD in U.S. economic history, and his MBA in economics from New York University. His teaching and research interests are in the evolution of economic theory and the formulation of macroeconomic and financial policies, with a focus on Political Economy. Prior to his academic work he was for 40 years a senior corporate executive and Chief Financial Officer in New York investment and commercial banking, including insurance, real estate, and government finance. He has published articles on historical finance, and his first book *The Power to Persuade: F.D.R., the Newsmagazines, and Going to War 1939–1941* was published in 2005. *Becoming the Arsenal*, an analysis of the American industrial mobilization for World War II, will be published in the winter of 2009–2010.

Tatiana Maksimenko is a PhD candidate in finance at the Zicklin School of Business, Baruch College, CUNY, where her research is in the field of financial intermediation and corporate finance. Previously, she was at the economic research department of the Federal Reserve Bank of Cleveland. She received her MBA in Finance at Weatherhead School of Management, Case Western Reserve University, and holds a BS in economics and mathematics from Novosibirsk State University, Russia. She has contributed to the textbook, *Micro Markets: A Market Structure Approach to Microeconomic Analysis.*